Kentucky Bourbon

Kentucky Bourbon

The Early Years of Whiskeymaking

Henry G. Crowgey

THE UNIVERSITY PRESS OF KENTUCKY

Scholarly publisher for the Commonwealth,
serving Bellarmine University, Berea College, Centre College of Kentucky,
Eastern Kentucky University, The Filson Historical Society, Georgetown
College, Kentucky Historical Society, Kentucky State University, Morehead
State University, Murray State University, Northern Kentucky University,
Transylvania University, University of Kentucky, University of Louisville,
and Western Kentucky University.
All rights reserved.

Editorial and Sales Offices: The University Press of Kentucky
663 South Limestone Street, Lexington, Kentucky 40508-4008
www.kentuckypress.com

Library of Congress Cataloging-in-Publication Data

Crowgey, Henry G.
  Kentucky bourbon : the early years of whiskeymaking / Henry G. Crowgey.
      p. cm.
  Originally published: Lexington : University Press of Kentucky, 1971.
  Includes bibliographical references and index.
  ISBN 978-0-8131-9183-6 (pbk. : alk. paper)
  1. Whiskey—Kentucky—History. 2. Distilling industries—Kentucky—History.
  I. Title.
  TP605.C76 2007
  663'.5209769—dc22   2007045738

This book is printed on acid-free recycled paper meeting the requirements of the
American National Standard for Permanence in Paper for Printed Library Materials.

Manufactured in the United States of America.

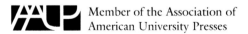 Member of the Association of
American University Presses

To My Mother

Contents

Acknowledgments

Since a substantial portion of this study first saw the light of day a number of years ago, a good many of the obligations to institutions and individuals have already been acknowledged. Nevertheless, there remains to this day a personal sense of indebtedness for innumerable favors which I am once more privileged to recognize, at least partially.

First of all, I am exceedingly grateful to the personnel of the Filson Club Library and the Special Collections Division of the University of Kentucky Library. In both cases the assistance and cooperation rendered invariably exceeded the bounds of routine duty. Once again, I would like to recognize those distilleries of Kentucky whose personnel have been uniformly cooperative in supplying factual information, both current and historical. In particular I am indebted to individuals from the following firms: Barton, Brown-Forman, Canada Dry, Medley, Old Taylor, Star Hill, Stitzel-Weller, and Willett. Several individuals who have been unusually generous with assistance and information are Paul Beasley, Jacqueline Bull, B. C. Campbell, Jr., Thomas T. Gray, Tommy Hamilton, O. M. Hawkins, Don Hynes, Jack Lancaster, John Medley, Marge Plamp, Frank Rankin, Julian VanWinkle, Jr., and Thompson Willett. Last, but by no means least, I shall always be indebted to Dr. Thomas D. Clark, former chairman of the History Department, University of Kentucky, for his invaluable advice and encouragement on all occasions.

Introduction

BOURBON WHISKEY, for all the parochialism its name might imply, is most of all a distinctive national product, unique to its native land. On May 4, 1964, the United States Congress recognized it as such, and Senate Concurrent Resolution 19 makes this clear:

That it is the sense of Congress that the recognition of Bourbon whiskey as a distinctive product of the United States be brought to the attention of the appropriate agencies of the United States Government toward the end that such agencies will take appropriate action to prohibit the importation into the United States of whisky [sic] designated as "Bourbon whiskey."[1]

Appropriately, this resolution was introduced by two congressmen from the state which produced in the following year (1965) approximately 71 percent of the whiskey made in the United States—Senator Thruston Morton and Representative John C. Watts of Kentucky.[2]

This admirable whiskey did not, of course, arrive in America as a sudden and brilliant invention, but resulted from a slowly maturing, ever-improving evolution from the expedients and experiments of the earliest colonists. For this reason, no small portion of this book is devoted to bourbon's early pedigree and worthy cousins in Virginia and the other colonies. To an amazing degree, the history of whiskey is a lively mirror to the manners and customs of the colonial time. Indeed, surveying the surviving documents of the American frontier, one can hardly fail to be impressed by the pervasiveness of strong drink in our nation's history.

For all that, the background of Kentucky whiskey is shaded in legend and myth. Many are the printed statements relative to the Kentucky background of bourbon whiskey which have inadequate or nonexistent factual bases. To the writer's knowledge, there has never been a carefully researched study relating to the early phases of distilling in Kentucky. This historical omission embraces a period of more than fifty years and includes nearly a full decade (1773–1782) of settlement activity for which no coverage exists—documented or otherwise. The situation can be partially explained by a lack of emphasis on contemporary personal accounts; with the exception of such preserved records as weekly newspapers (beginning in 1787), court proceedings, and a few travel accounts, there is an undeniable paucity of reliable information. This, however, cannot be attributed solely to backwoods illiteracy or the pressures and preoccupations of pioneer life.

It is possible, and indeed somewhat likely, that some of the records of early distilling have been eradicated by the descendants of the distillers. The temperance movement reached full force in the nineteenth century and its adherents would have viewed such a family background as an opprobrium. It can hardly be mere accident that so many personal reminiscences and accounts of a biographical nature tend to omit reference to the production or consumption of distilled products, when the facts are known to be otherwise.[3]

[1] U. S., *Statutes at Large*, 78:1208.

[2] U. S., *Congressional Record*, 110, part 7:9703–05; part 8:9962–64. Representative John C. Watts was from the Sixth Congressional District of Kentucky, which included Bourbon County. Charles B. Brownson, comp., *Congressional Staff Directory, 1964* (Washington, D.C., 1964), 23, 24. Figures relating to Kentucky whiskey production are from Charles B. Garrison, *Impact of the Distilled Spirits Production Tax on Kentucky's Economy* (Lexington, 1965), 30.

[3] See, for example, Cassius Marcellus Clay, *The Life of Cassius Marcel-*

Several of the Kentucky counties have practically disowned any previous affiliation with the one industry that was probably most responsible for any early prosperity which they may have enjoyed. From a total of one hundred and twenty counties in the state, eighty-six were completely dry as of September 1967; paradoxically, distilleries were located in two of these dry counties.[4] The stepchild aspect of distilling is perfectly illustrated in the case of the one county—Bourbon—which logically should, above all others, pay tribute to the product that was so valuable in the formative years and which became the county's namesake. In connection with anniversary celebrations of their founding, the town of Paris and the county of Bourbon each published a pamphlet containing some description of the area's history. For its sesquicentennial celebration, the former recognized native sons in the person of educators, explorers, judges, politicians, publishers, authors, ministers, inventors, and printers. However, save for the lone reference to John Hamilton (1795), there is no mention of the early distillers.[5] The county publication, alluding to 175 years of existence, devoted about half a page to early distilling and mentioned only three of the persons directly connected with it.[6] Equally puzzling is the fact that this county has not seen fit to capitalize on an obvious opportunity; there are no active distilleries in Bourbon County at the present writing.

Practically none of the modern-day references to the early industry are in complete agreement on the factual particulars of

---

lus Clay: Memoirs, Writings and Speeches (Cincinnati, 1886). His father, General Green Clay, was one of the biggest distillers of early Kentucky; yet the author never mentions this fact.

[4] Interview with Porter Collier, director, Field Division, Kentucky State Alcoholic Beverage Control Department, September 14, 1967. See also Louisville Courier-Journal, September 15, 1967.

[5] Julia Hoge Ardery, Paris (Hopewell) Sesquicentennial: A Record of the One Hundred and Fiftieth Anniversary of the Founding of Bourbon's County Seat (Paris, Ky., 1939).

[6] Bourbon County Historical Scrapbook: A Record of the Celebration of the One Hundred Seventy-fifth Anniversary of the Founding of Bourbon County, Kentucky (Paris, Ky., 1961).

the Kentucky beginnings. There is no apparent consensus on the identity of the first distiller of the state, nor on the specific origins of bourbon whiskey with regard to material or method. There is not even a general concurrence in the spelling of the generic word —"whisky" and "whiskey" are used indiscriminately, apparently in accordance with individual preference, as was done in earlier days. The thirsty frontiersman of eighteenth-century Kentucky certainly had little concern for the spelling of his favorite beverage; this is equally true of his twentieth-century descendants. Many writers have followed this practice, with numerous examples of the interchanged spelling in evidence throughout their work; Mrs. Frances Trollope allowed several of such interchanges in her description of the Americans and their "domestic manners."[7]

The present investigation is almost exclusively devoted to the first half-century of Kentucky distilling, with a certain amount of additional emphasis on those first few years of settlement which have been completely ignored by the early historians in their guarded mention of whiskey and distillers. This chronological delimitation, though not completely arbitrary, allows concentration in the area where coverage has been most inadequate. The years succeeding the period under study have had considerably more attention; there are accounts of the beginnings of several company operations which extend back to the period immediately preceding the Civil War.[8]

The author has permitted himself some latitude in describing the alcoholic predilections of the early American colonists, for the tastes and manners of the Kentucky pioneers derived from the

[7] Frances Trollope, *Domestic Manners of the Americans* (London, 1839), 39, 77, 325, 327, 357. Several works contain the interchanged spellings on the same page; see, for example, Michael August Krafft, *The American Distiller* (Philadelphia, 1804), 104; Ben Casseday, *The History of Louisville from Its Earliest Settlement Till the Year 1852* (Louisville, 1852), 27; Daniel Drake, *Pioneer Life in Kentucky, 1785–1800*, ed. Emmet Field Horine (New York, 1948), 84.

[8] Sam Carpenter Elliott, *Nelson County Record: An Illustrated Historical and Industrial Supplement* (Bardstown, 1896).

older settlements of the Atlantic seaboard, and particularly from the areas which furnished most of Kentucky's settlers—Virginia, Pennsylvania, Maryland, and North Carolina. Here originated the interest in liquor, the equipment, and the techniques which later brought fame and prosperity to the Kentucky distillers.

KENTUCKY BOURBON

1

Thirsty Colonists

THE ART OF DISTILLING was introduced into Europe in
the twelfth century by way of Egypt and Moorish Spain and
spread rapidly throughout the continent.[1] Its introduction into the
adjacent British Isles during the thirteenth century has often been
credited to that celebrated friar, Roger Bacon.[2] A familiarity with
distilling, together with a penchant for the product, accompanied
the colonists from England to the shores of America in 1607. The
early Virginians, and indeed the settlers in all the Atlantic colonies,
soon found ways to convert indigenous materials of fruit and
grain into spirituous drink. A taste for alcoholic beverages was an
ingrained characteristic of all colonizing nations of the seventeenth
century.

Two handicaps confronted the early distillers—the absence of
sophisticated apparatus and their unfamiliarity with the raw
materials available in this new land. The colonists directed their
first efforts toward crude forms of fermented beverages such as
beer, ale, and wine. Thomas Hariot of the short-lived Roanoke
Island colony reported that "Wee made of the same [mayze] in
the countrey some mault, whereof was brued as good ale as was to
bee desired. So likewise by the help of hops thereof may bee made
as good Beere."[3] The first colonists at Jamestown also discovered
native maize and Captain John Smith chronicled the "toyle" involved in preparing the ground to plant "corne" in 1607.[4] Wild
grapes were one of the native fruits the colonists found in abun-

dance, and the English, being familiar with the fruit of the vine, accordingly wasted no time in exploiting this product. William Strachey wrote favorably in 1610 of having "drunck often of the . . . wine which . . . our people have made full as good, as your French British wyne."[5] He also noted a handicap to production: "Twenty gallons at a tyme have bene sometimes made without any other helpe then by crushing the grape with the hand, which letting to settle five or six daies, hath, in the drawing forth, proved strong and headdy."[6] By 1620, one of the colonists could write to a friend in England that they were making a drink from Indian corn which he preferred to English beer.[7]

In one instance Strachey commented on the dearth of fruit such as "peares and apples [which] they have none to make syder or perry of," but later perceptively noted the indigenous "crabb trees there be, . . . howbeit, being graffed upon, soone might we have of our owne apples of any kind, peares, and what ells."[8] This nostalgic observation was soon acted upon, for by 1629 there were "Peaches in abundance at *Kecoughtan*. Apples, Peares, Apricocks, Vines, figges, and other fruits some have been planted that prospered exceedingly."[9] Generally speaking, all of these

[1] Adam Anderson, *An Historical and Chronological Deduction of the Origin of Commerce, from the Earliest Accounts* (London, 1787–1789), 1:xxxiii, 154.

[2] R. Vashon Rogers, *Drinks, Drinkers and Drinking, or the Law and History of Intoxicating Liquors* (Albany, 1881), 16.

[3] Thomas Hariot, *Narrative of the First English Plantation of Virginia* (Reprint of 1588 edition; London, 1893), 21–22.

[4] John Smith, *The Generall Historie of Virginia, New-England, and the Summer Isles* . . . (London, 1632), 42; Lyon Gardiner Tyler, ed., *Narratives of Early Virginia, 1606–1625*, in *Original Narratives of Early American History*, ed. J. Franklin Jameson (19 vols.; New York, 1906–1917), 35.

[5] William Strachey, *The Historie of Travaile into Virginia Britannia* (Reprint of manuscript copy, c. 1618; London, 1899), 120.

[6] Ibid.

[7] Philip Alexander Bruce, *Economic History of Virginia in the Seventeenth Century* (New York, 1907), 2:212 n.

[8] Strachey, *Historie of Travaile*, 74, 130.

[9] Edward Arber, ed., *Travels and Works of Captain John Smith: President of Virginia, and Admiral of New England, 1580–1631* (Edinburgh, 1910), 2:887.

fruits were highly eligible materials for distillation into brandy, just as the colonists' corn beer was adaptable to conversion into corn liquor. In somewhat over two decades on the American continent, the settlers were successfully practicing fermentation with homegrown products and were but one step removed from the manufacture of their own distilled spirits.

The free use of intoxicants by Virginians is evidenced by a law passed in 1619 at the first session of the General Assembly:

Against drunkenness be it also decreed that if any private person be found culpable thereof, for the first time he is to be reprooved privately by the Minister, the second time publiquely, the thirde time to lye in boltes 12 howers in the house of the Provost Marshall and to paye his fee, and if he still continue in that vice, to undergo suche severe punishment as the Governor and Counsell of Estate shall thinke fitt to be inflicted on him.[10]

A legislative act of 1645 forbade any person's taking "for the best sorte of all English strong waters above the rate of 80 lb. of tobacco per gall. and for aqua vitae or brandy above the rate of 40 lb. tob'o per gallon."[11] In addition to providing an early example of price control, the legislation suggests that Virginians were distilling fruit brandies well before the middle of the seventeenth century.

Assembly legislation in 1666 was even more specific: "for Virginia drams [locally produced apple and peach brandy] the like prices as for brandy and English spiritts."[12] The inventory of a York County, Virginia, store (1667), following the death of the owner, showed that among the contents were "one hundred gallons of brandy, twenty gallons of wine, and ten gallons of aqua vitae."[13] An account of Governor Spotswood's crossing of the Blue Ridge Mountains provides some indication of the selection that was

[10] Tyler, *Narratives of Early Virginia*, 263.

[11] William Waller Hening, comp., *The Statutes at Large: being a Collection of all the Laws of Virginia, from the First Session of the Legislature, in the Year 1619* (Imprint varies, 1819–1823), 1:300.

[12] Ibid., 2:234.

[13] Bruce, *Economic History of Virginia*, 2:382.

3

available to the Virginians in 1716: "we had several sorts of liquors, viz., Virginia red wine and white wine, Irish usquebaugh, brandy, shrub, two sorts of rum, champagne, canary, cherry, punch, water, cider, &c."[14] Quite possibly the governor was suffering from a fit of absent-mindedness when he included the prosaic "water" in his list of this enticing assortment of colonial beverages.

Robert Beverley supplied some indication of the source of these items in his colorful history of the colony: "Their strong drink is Madera Wine, Cyder, Mobby Punch, made either of Rum from the *Caribbee* Islands, or Brandy distill'd from their Apples and Peaches; besides Brandy, Wine, and strong Beer, which they have constantly from *England*."[15] He then added a very informative description of the horticultural and distillation practices involved in this domestic production:

The Fruit-Trees [apples] are wonderfully quick of Growth; so that in six or seven Years time from the Planting, a Man may bring an Orchard to bear in great Plenty, from which he may make Store of good Cyder, or distill great Quantities of Brandy; for the Cyder is very strong, and yields abundance of Spirit. . . . [Peaches] commonly bear in three Years from the Stone, . . . others make a Drink of them, which they call Mobby, and either drink it as Cyder, or distill it off for Brandy. This makes the best Spirit next to Grapes.[16]

With but slight variation in literary construction, the preceding quotation might have been written some 250 years later—and be similarly applicable in the technical sense!

The seventeenth century marked the establishment of distilling in the other Atlantic colonies as well. Traditionally, New Englanders are considered to have specialized in rum manufacture.

---

[14] Ann Maury, ed., *Memoirs of a Huguenot Family* (Reprint of original edition of 1852; New York, 1853), 289. Contains "Journal" of John Fontaine, who accompanied Governor Spotswood.

[15] Robert Beverley, *The History of Virginia, in Four Parts* (London, 1722), 254.

[16] Ibid., 278–79.

4

However, their early pattern of development in distilling closely paralleled that of the Virginians. One of the earliest (and most entertaining) accounts of spirituous liquors is that of the celebrated *bon vivant*, Thomas Morton. In 1628, on the shores of Boston Bay, he and his fun-loving followers scandalized their Plymouth neighbors by "quaffing and drinking both wine and strong waters in great exsess . . . 10 *li* [pounds] worth in a morning."[17] Morton's own account of the festivities indicates that local production played a considerable part in the provisioning of the affair. They "brewed a barrell of excellent beare and provided a case of bottles, to be spent, with other good cheare, for all commers of that day."[18] Governor Bradford's chronicle provides an indication of the prevailing Puritan attitude toward "strong drinck." Although he admits to a distaste for the scandalous overindulgence, he also implies that Morton's truly unpardonable sin was selling firearms to his Indian friends.[19]

The foregoing account does not specifically refer to any distilling in New England at the time, but by mid-century there is no question about its existence. A legal transaction of 1654 in Boston establishes William Toy as being a distiller.[20] The historian J. Leander Bishop reports that by 1661 a still and worm had been set up in New London "for distilling rum from the molasses procured there in exchange for the exports of the Colony."[21]

Immediately to the south of New England, other European immigrants were likewise importing the art of distilling to their adopted country. The Dutch West India colony of New Netherlands established an historic distillery in the area of present-day

[17] William T. Davis, ed., *Bradford's History of Plymouth Plantation, 1606–1646*, in *Original Narratives of Early American History*, ed. J. Franklin Jameson (19 vols.; New York, 1906–1917), 238.

[18] Charles Francis Adams, Jr., ed., *The New England Canaan of Thomas Morton* (Boston, 1883), 276.

[19] Davis, *Bradford's History*, 238.

[20] Henry J. Kauffman, *Early American Copper, Tin and Brass* (New York, 1950), 54.

[21] J. Leander Bishop, *A History of American Manufactures from 1608 to 1860* (Philadelphia, 1864), 1:51.

New York City. Opinions vary regarding the exact site and the product manufactured, but two authorities are in agreement on the date. Edward Emerson places the operation on Staten Island and identifies the product as liquor and spirits from corn and rye.[22] Bishop locates the distillery in the Wall Street area and states that it produced brandy.[23] Both consider this as the first instance of its kind in North America and the date of its establishment as 1640. There is evidence that the neighboring colony of New Sweden was also interested in the production of liquor. Governor Johan Rising's report to the Swedish Commercial College in 1654 enumerated the facilities needed to produce a flourishing colony; these included "brewery and distillery, and alehouses."[24] Quite possibly the nearby Dutch distillery was so successful that the Swedes were envious.

An abundance of records supports the existence of distilling activity in the New York area during the latter half of the seventeenth century. A distiller of 1665, Raynier vander Cooley, received official permission to move from the Delaware River area to New York "with his Stills, Vessells, and any other necessaryes belonging to him, or his Trade."[25] The misuse of distilled products is apparent in the recommendation of a Delaware-area official, submitted to the New York governor in 1671: "That y° distilling of Strong Liquo." out of Corne, being y° Cause of a great Consumption of that Graine, as also of y° Debauchery & Idleness of y° Inhabitants, from whence inevitably will follow their Poverty & Ruine, bee absolutely prohibited or restrayned."[26]

In 1672 the English governor, Francis Lovelace, received a

[22] Edward R. Emerson, *Beverages, Past and Present* (New York, 1908), 2:463.

[23] Bishop, *History of American Manufactures*, 1:250.

[24] Albert Cook Myers, ed., *Narratives of Early Pennsylvania, West New Jersey, and Delaware, 1630–1707*, in *Original Narratives of Early American History*, ed. J. Franklin Jameson (19 vols.; New York, 1906–1917), 141.

[25] Victor Hugo Paltsits, ed., *Minutes of the Executive Council of the Province of New York, 1668–1673* (Albany, 1910), 1:179 n.

[26] Ibid., 2:559.

6

petition from a woman in the Delaware River area who was "wont to distill some small quantities of liquors from corn" and desired "license to distill in her own distilling kettle."[27]

In Eastern Pennsylvania, a court order of 1676 illustrates both the importance of grain to the early settlers and the extent to which distilling was practiced. The distilling of any grain was prohibited unless it be "unfit to grind and boalt."[28] Distilling by the early Pennsylvanians was not limited to grain, however, and their versatility was chronicled by Gabriel Thomas in his account of "Pensilvania and of West-New-Jersey" in 1698. In addition to making "much excellent Cyder" of apples, they also had "Pears, Peaches, etc. of which they distil a Liquor much like the taste of Rumm, or Brandy, which they Yearly make in great quantities."[29]

In Maryland the pattern was similar to that in Virginia, with early plantings of fruit trees. By the end of the seventeenth century a varied assortment of orchard produce was available for conversion into spirits. A traveler to Maryland in 1705 recorded "[an] abundance of fruits of all sorts as aple Peare Cherry quinces in great quantities and innumerable Quantities Peaches to that degree that they knock downe Bushells att a time for there hogs, besides what vast quantities they still and make a verry good spirritt off nott much inferior to Brandy."[30]

In the Carolina settlements (chartered in 1663), the early population was derived principally from Virginia and the settlers followed the patterns set by older colonies. In 1682, Thomas Ashe visited the Charles Town area of the Carolinas and reported on the use of Indian corn in producing alcoholic beverages: "At Carolina they have lately invented a way of making with it good sound Beer: but its strong and heady: By Maceration, when duly fermented, a strong Spirit like Brandy may be drawn off from it, by

---

[27] Emerson, *Beverages, Past and Present*, 2:463.

[28] Bishop, *History of American Manufactures*, 1:140.

[29] Myers, *Narratives of Early Pennsylvania*, 323.

[30] As quoted in Margaret Shove Morriss, *Colonel Trade of Maryland, 1689–1715*, Johns Hopkins University Studies in Historical and Political Science, 32, no. 3 (Baltimore, 1914): 18.

the help of an Alembick [still]."[31] In the northern sector, now North Carolina, the widespread consumption of liquor, accompanied by overindulgence, prompted an Act of Assembly in 1715 for the purpose of regulating "ordinary Keepers and Tippling houses."[32] The North Carolina historian R. D. W. Connor estimated that "by the middle of the eighteenth century distilling had come to be considered one of the chief industries of the colony."[33]

A perceptive visitor to North Carolina from Ireland, Dr. John Brickell, provided an interesting account of drinking habits in that colony in about 1737:

> For I have frequently seen them come to the Towns, and there remain Drinking Rum, Punch, and other Liquors for Eight or Ten Days successively, and after they have committed this Excess, will not drink any Spirituous Liquor, 'till such time as they take *the next Frolick*, as they call it, which is generally in two or three Months. . . . But amongst the better Sort, or those of good OEconomy, it is quite otherwise, who seldom frequent the Taverns, having plenty of Wine, Rum, and other Liquors at their own Houses. . . . The former sometimes bring their Wives with them to be pertakers of these Frolicks, which very often is not commendable or decent to behold.[34]

His observation concerning the two classes of settlers is similar to that of others who have noted the class differences in drinking habits and types of beverages used. Lewis Gray in his excellent summary of the entire colonial period writes, "Production of the common English fruits for home use early became very general. The use of various beverages made from fruit, such as perry, peach, and other brandies, and cider, was very general. While the

---

[31] Alexander S. Salley, Jr., ed., *Narratives of Early Carolina, 1650–1708,* in *Original Narratives of Early American History,* ed. J. Franklin Jameson (19 vols.; New York, 1906–1917), 145.

[32] Coralie Parker, *The History of Taxation in North Carolina during the Colonial Period, 1663–1776* (New York, 1928), 129.

[33] R. D. W. Connor, *North Carolina: Rebuilding an Ancient Commonwealth, 1584–1925* (Chicago, 1929), 1:210.

[34] John Brickell, *The Natural History of North Carolina* (Dublin, 1737), 33–34.

wealthier planters imported foreign wines, the masses depended
on the various domestic drinks, including those distilled from
fruit juices."[35] For the most part, it was this latter class, from
Virginia (principally), Maryland, North Carolina, and Pennsylvania, which settled in Kentucky in the final three decades of the
eighteenth century, bringing with them long-established habits
regarding the distillation of strong liquors from both fruits and
grains. They retained also their attitude toward the use of spirits
as a way of life, as a necessity for almost all social occasions. The
ubiquitous presence of liquor in social affairs is copiously illustrated in contemporary accounts.

The importance of liquid refreshments in one aspect of colonial
life is strikingly illustrated by reviewing the accounts of burials
and, on occasion, the accompanying mortuary expenses. At a
Virginia funeral in 1667, some twenty-two gallons of cider, five
gallons of brandy, and twenty-four gallons of beer were consumed
in paying appropriate homage to the departed relative's memory.[36]
At another Virginia funeral (Washington County) the cost of
refreshments seems to have been the major expense: "13¼ gallons
of Whiskey [@] 10/ per gallon, 6/12/6; plank & winding sheet
1/11/0."[37] The versatile Englishman, Nicholas Cresswell, attended a funeral in West Augusta, Virginia, in 1775. He "performed the part of a Clergyman at the funeral of an infant" and
noted that "at the Grave the parents and friends Wept and drank
Whiskey alternately."[38] Colonial mourners in North Carolina seem
also to have required spirituous comfort: "There was much eating
and drinking. Seven gallons of whiskey were drunk at a funeral in
Mecklenburg County in 1767, at the expense of the estate."[39]

Not everyone approved of such practices. A York County,

[35] Lewis Cecil Gray, *History of Agriculture in the Southern United States to 1860* (New York, 1941), 1:190.

[36] Bruce, *Economic History of Virginia*, 2:236.

[37] Washington County, Virginia, Will Book No. 1, 1777–1792, 118.

[38] Nicholas Cresswell, *The Journal of Nicholas Cresswell, 1774–1777* (London, 1925), 123.

[39] Hugh Talmage Lefler, ed., *North Carolina History Told by Contemporaries* (Chapel Hill, 1948), 81.

Virginia, bequest of the late seventeenth century directed: "Having observed in the dais of my pilgrimage the debauches used at burialls tending much to the dishonour of God and his true Religion, my will is that noe strong drinke bee p'vided or spirits at my burialls."[40]

Recorded wills and estate inventories provide evidence of the importance attached to both the distilling apparatus and its product. The will of Matthew Rust of Westmoreland County, Virginia, (1751) provided that his "still worm & Tub" should go to a son; to another son he devised "a still that will work fifty Gallons with worm & Tubb."[41] Benjamin Rust, of the adjacent Richmond County, either had no sons to carry on the distillery business or else desired to provide his daughter with an irresistible dowry. His will, executed in 1754, provided that she should receive 750 acres, a Negro woman, "all my home Stock of Cattle hoggs & sheep and all my horses my Still & worm, and all my household furniture."[42]

In North Carolina, a Bertie County citizen in 1759 bequeathed his copper still to his four sons, stipulating "that they shall still all their Mothers Liquor during her life."[43] An inhabitant of western North Carolina dispensed with his still while living but executed a bond for his own support by the recipients, his two sons. One stipulation was that they furnish him with twelve gallons of whiskey each year.[44] In these colonial settings, the culture and economy were rural at best and often backwoods in character. Hence a still and its necessary appurtenances, representing a considerable monetary investment, might comprise the single most

[40] Bruce, *Economic History of Virginia*, 2:217.

[41] Ellsworth Marshall Rust, ed., *Rust of Virginia* (Washington, 1940), 47–48. "Worm" refers to the tubular coil of metal—usually copper—leading from the top (or head) of the still. The alcoholic steam is conducted through this water-cooled worm and thereby condensed into liquid spirits.

[42] Ibid., 50–51.

[43] Connor, *North Carolina*, 1:211.

[44] Joseph R. Nixon, *The German Settlers in Lincoln County and Western North Carolina*, James Sprunt Historical Publications of the North Carolina Historical Society, 11, no. 2 (Chapel Hill, 1912): 42.

valuable asset in a person's worldly estate. This is evident in the wording of another western North Carolina will of pre-Revolution days: "I leave the still for the benefit of the family whilst my wife keeps house with the children."[45]

The complete acceptance of spirituous liquors by colonial society is nowhere better illustrated than by the attitude of the frontier clergy. In the early records of Virginia, there is considerable evidence of overindulgence by members of the cloth. The 1631 session of the General Assembly recognized this state of affairs with the admonition that "mynisters shall not give themselves to excesse in drinkinge, or riott."[46] Further regulation of clerical social behavior was provided by the Assembly in 1676, with a fine of "the one halfe of one yeares sallary" for "such ministers as shall become notoriously scandulous by drunkingnesse . . . or other haynous and crying sins."[47] In North Carolina, Connor reports that an "Anglican missionary was denounced by Governor Everhard [1725–1731] as 'a scandalous drunken man.' "[48]

Somewhat more commercial in their approach to distilled spirits were the Moravians of present-day Forsyth County, North Carolina. In November and December of 1756 they erected a log house to serve as a combination bakery and distillery.[49] An entry in the records of this efficiently run enterprise discloses that on May 3, 1776, "distilling stopped today. Twenty-one hundred gallons of brandy were made during the past winter."[50] Considering the amount of their production and the fact that a tavern was operated in conjunction with the distillery, these people had surprisingly little trouble with intemperance among their members. On one occasion the Conference decreed that "brandy shall be kept

[45] Ibid.

[46] Hening, *Statutes at Large*, 1:158.

[47] Ibid., 384.

[48] Connor, *North Carolina*, 1:210.

[49] Adelaide L. Fries, ed., *Records of the Moravians in North Carolina, 1752–1822* (Raleigh, 1922–1954), 1:160–61.

[50] Ibid., 3:1096.

away from C. F. who does not know how to use it in moderation."[51] There are very few such instances in the Moravian annals, and the standard remedy seems to have been, in every case, enforced abstention.

With noteworthy realism, the early German Lutherans of Lincoln County, North Carolina, seem also to have accepted the colonial facts of life, for one "distinguished minister of the gospel, among other items of maintenance, required that his wife be furnished on January first of each and every year 'ten gallons of good whiskey.' "[52]

The relationship between the frontier Methodist clergy and spirituous liquor is recorded by Peter Cartwright in his autobiography. He first praises the "far-seeing wisdom of John Wesley" for interdicting dram-drinking in his General Rules, "while the whole religious world, priests, preachers, and members rushed into this demoralizing practice."[53] Cartwright then comments on the "dead letter" aspect of such attempted regulatory measures by adding a full-scale description of frontier drinking habits:

From my earliest recollection drinking drams, in family and social circles, was considered harmless and allowable sociality. It was almost universally the custom for preachers, in common with all others, to take drams; and if a man would not have it in his family, his harvest, his house-raisings, log-rollings, weddings, and so on, he was considered parsimonious and unsociable; and many, even professors of Christianity, would not help a man if he did not have spirits and treat the company.[54]

In frontier western Pennsylvania the attitude of the religious groups was permissive toward distilled spirits but utterly unbending toward questionable business ethics. One communicant was excluded by the church governing body for selling whiskey "which

---

[51] Ibid., 5:2099.
[52] Connor, *North Carolina*, 1:211.
[53] Peter Cartwright, *The Backwoods Preacher: An Autobiography* (London, 1858), 119.
[54] Ibid.

froze in the bottle." Following an admission that he had put a "small quantity of water into his last bbl.," and a suitable expression of repentance, he was duly rebuked, admonished, and restored to his former standing.[55] The inclination to increase production by the addition of water must have been a general shortcoming of colonials engaged in the manufacture and sale of strong drink. At any rate it was not solely a Pennsylvania practice, nor were attempts at control limited to the clergy. The Virginia Assembly in 1645 enacted legislation to prevent fraudulent mixing or corrupting of wines or strong waters.[56]

Still other facets of colonial life in the central Atlantic colonies testify to the important position occupied by distilling and the "cradle to grave" application of its products. Strong spirits were one of the components in all stocks of materia medica, often the principal ingredient in prescriptions, regardless of the patient's age. Quite possibly the alcoholic effect was the sole benefit—real or imagined. Colonel Landon Carter's diary of life in mid-eighteenth-century Virginia provides many examples of the blind faith in alcohol-based concoctions prescribed for gastric ailments. The colonel relates that on one occasion, plagued with an upset stomach, "to prevent the Sickness I joined about 2 teaspoonfuls of brandy and a lump or two sugar."[57] In a recipe "to strengthen the Stomach" he recommends "2 teaspoonfulls of tincture of bark made with a full ounce if not two of a pint of brandy."[58] With or without the additive, a two-ounce dose of homemade brandy, repeated at frequent intervals, should have alleviated most discomforts.

One of the earliest and most effective of remedies—certainly one of the most original—was reported by Captain John Smith

[55] Marian Silveus, "Churches and Social Control on the Western Pennsylvania Frontier," *Western Pennsylvania Historical Magazine* 19 (June 1936): 132.

[56] Hening, *Statutes at Large*, 1:300.

[57] Jack P. Greene, ed., *The Diary of Colonel Landon Carter of Sabine Hall, 1752–1778* (Charlottesville, 1965), 2:866.

[58] Ibid., 838.

in the case of "a Salvage smoothered at Jamestown." The patient in this instance had been overcome by smoke while confined in a dungeon, and the prescribed remedy was liberal application (internally) of *aqua vitae* and vinegar." The resuscitative process was, if anything, overly successful; Smith described the revived savage as "so drunke & affrighted, that he seemed Lunaticke."[59]

Another application of medicinal firewater was chronicled by John Long, an Indian trader of the late 1770s. On this occasion the patient was a drunken Indian woman whose unruly behavior exhausted the trader's patience. He "infused forty drops of the tincture cantharides, and the same quantity of laudanum, into a glass of rum . . . gave her the dose . . . [which] made her stagger." A second application of this frontier Mickey Finn finished the victim who "fell on the floor. . . . [where] she remained twelve hours in a deep sleep . . . making the life of a trader more tolerable, by putting a stop to their impertinence."[60]

From the onset of colonization by Old World inhabitants, their relations with the naive aborigines were constantly marred by the introduction of strong drink. This had become a widespread practice by mid-seventeenth century. Israel Acrelius, the Swedish historian, commented on a 1654 council attended by ten Indian chiefs; both wine and brandy were liberally distributed to the gullible natives.[61] The colonial records of New York show that Indians were frequently given spirits as partial payment for labor performed. This was an officially sanctioned practice, as is illustrated in a memorandum of 1672: "That John Cooper may have Lycense to furnish his Indyans wth a Gyll of Liquo'' now & then as occasion shall require, placing it to ye Acco^t of part paym^t of their Wages."[62]

[59] Smith, *Generall Historie of Virginia*, 85.

[60] Reuben Gold Thwaites, ed., *Early Western Travels, 1748–1846* (Cleveland, 1904–1907), 2:149. Long's inclusion of an aphrodisiac in his "prescription" casts some doubt upon the purity of his intent.

[61] Israel Acrelius, *A History of New Sweden: or, The Settlements on the River Delaware*, trans. William M. Reynolds (Philadelphia, 1876), 64.

[62] Paltsits, *Executive Council*, 2:474.

Early colonial laws pertaining to Indian relations often reflect the disparity between governmental pronouncements and the realities of frontier existence. A Virginia law of 1705 provided a ten shilling fine "for every quart of rum, or brandy sold to any Indian."[63] Another enactment in 1757 was designed to control trade with the "Indians in alliance with His Majesty" by appointing trustees to contract with the traders. Included in the instructions was the following limitation: "Said trustees shall not send out, or permit or suffer to be sent out, any rum, brandy, or other spirituous liquors to be bartered or sold to such Indians by any such factor or factors, or other persons by them employed for carrying on the said trade."[64]

Despite these altruistic measures, there was apparently no real restriction. In 1754 George Croghan's trip took him to Log's Town (the scene of Braddock's defeat a year and a half later) "where we found the Indians all drunk."[65] This observation is almost identical to that of Christian Frederick Post on a trip to the Ohio for the governor of Pennsylvania in 1758. He "proceeded as far as German Town, where I found all the Indians drunk."[66]

The pernicious effect of liquor was recognized by a few responsible Indian leaders who tried, though ineffectively, to restrict its availability. A Catawba king in North Carolina eloquently summarized the situation at a conference in 1754:

Brothers here is One thing You yourselves are to Blame very much in, That is You Rot Your grain in Tubs, out of which you take and make Strong Spirits You sell it to our young men and give it to them, many times; they get very Drunk . . . this is the Very Cause that they oftentimes Commit those Crimes that is offencive to You and us and all thro' the Effect of that Drink it is also very bad for our people, for it Rots their guts and Causes our men to get very sick and many of our people has Lately Died by the Effects of that strong Drink, and I heartily wish You

[63] Hening, *Statutes at Large*, 3:468.
[64] Ibid., 7:116–17.
[65] Thwaites, *Early Western Travels*, 1:74.
[66] Ibid., 184.

would do something to prevent Your People from Dareing to Sell or give them any of that Strong Drink, upon any Consideration whatever for that will be a great means of our being free from being accused of those Crimes that is Commited by our young men and will prevent many of the abuses that is done by them thro' the Effects of that Strong Drink.[67]

Obviously the Indians had no trouble in securing liquor despite prohibitory enactments, and the volume of the trade, along a frontier that extended from the Great Lakes to the Gulf of Mexico, must have been large indeed. Such a ready market for the product doubtless prompted untold scores of small, back-country distillers to engage in the business.

In addition to promoting frontier trade with the Indians, liquor flowed freely in early American political life. Realistic political candidates made it a rule not only to entertain their friends and potential supporters in advance of elections but also to hold open house for any qualified voter on his way to the polls. Quite often a barrel of free liquor was available on the grounds of the polling place.[68] Ungrateful indeed would have been the voter who, after partaking liberally of such an offering, failed to vote for the donor. Charles S. Sydnor makes the point that free liquor caused much rowdiness, fighting, and drunkenness but was a contribution to eighteenth-century democracy in that it induced voters to appear at the polls.[69]

In Frederick County, Virginia, Colonel George Washington stood for election to the House of Burgesses in 1758. Although Washington did not attend the hustings in person, his representatives ran up an amazing entertainment bill, considering the relatively small number who balloted. The successful Washington received a total of 307 votes. The expense account totaled thirty-eight pounds and seven shillings, of which over thirty-four pounds

---

[67] Lefler, *North Carolina History*, 73–74.
[68] Charles S. Sydnor, *Gentlemen Freeholders: Political Practices in Washington's Virginia* (Chapel Hill, 1952), 52–54.
[69] Ibid., 58–59.

was for brandy, rum, Cyder Royal, strong beer, and wine.[70]
The same practice prevailed at a Virginia election in 1777.
William C. Rives recounts: "Mr. [James] Madison was outvoted
by candidates who brought to their aid a species of influence unfortunately not uncommon in that day, but against which he was
firmly principled. The practice of *treating* at elections was one
which, in England, had long and rankly flourished in spite of
prohibitory enactments; and it had been transplanted, with the
representative institutions which it tended to vitiate and corrupt,
to the virgin soil of the new world."[71] The realities of political
life were indelibly impressed on Madison, for he later recalled
that "the people not only tolerated, but expected and even required
to be courted and treated, [and] no candidate, who neglected those
attentions, could be elected. . . . forebearance would have been
ascribed to a mean parsimony, or to a proud disrespect for the
voters."[72] Madison's latest biographer, Irving Brant, notes that
"there was only one decisive issue. Madison refused to give the
voters free whisky."[73]

The practice of treating was carried to such excesses that by
the early eighteenth century there were statutes to prohibit it.[74]
Colonel Landon Carter's privately kept journal of the House of
Burgesses refers to a case of this kind in 1752, and the legal side-
stepping that ensued. "Notwithstanding of Dewy's Son-in-Law
giving the Liquor that was brought to the Election . . . All the
time of Voting, yet, as it did not appear that Dewy ordered it, he
was duly Elected."[75]

[70] John C. Fitzpatrick, ed., *The Writings of George Washington from
the Original Manuscript Sources, 1745–1799* (Washington, D.C., 1931–
1941), 2:241–42 n.

[71] William C. Rives, *History of the Life and Times of James Madison*
(Boston, 1868–1873), 1:179.

[72] Irving Brant, *James Madison* (Indianapolis, 1941–1961), 1:306;
Rives, *James Madison*, 1:180.

[73] Brant, *James Madison*, 1:306.

[74] Hening, *Statutes at Large*, 3:243. As evidence that continuing attempts were made to legally disallow treating, see Hening, 9:57.

[75] Greene, *Diary of Landon Carter*, 1:89.

The significant use of liquor by the colonial Americans is nowhere better illustrated than by its consumption in the armed forces, both regulars and militia. The presence of military detachments in any area of the colonies occasioned a demand for spirits. In addition to the prescribed ration of liquor—usually one gill per day—extra rations were furnished for activities which exceeded the normal. General Washington acknowledged this practice in 1777: "It is necessary, there should always be a Sufficient Quantity of Spirits with the Army, to furnish moderate Supplies to the Troops. In many instances, such as when they are marching in hot or Cold weather, in Camp or Wet, on fatigue or in Working Parties, it is so essential that it is not to be dispensed with."[76] The general considered an adequate supply of strong liquor so important that, in a letter to the president of Congress, he recommended the erection of "Public Distilleries in different States," and the appointment of "proper persons to buy Grain and distill it for the Army."[77] To bolster this proposal, he asserted that "the benefits arising from the moderate use of strong Liquor, have been experienced in All Armies, and are not to be disputed."[78] His allusion to the use of liquor in "All Armies" is supported by a captured letter of David Lyster, of the British Royal Artillery under Governor Hamilton at Detroit. Writing to a friend in 1779, Lyster notes that "every man that works is allowed One Pint of Rum p' Day beside One Ration."[79]

Such requirements, if unsatisfied through normal channels, often led to the practice of impressment, as is illustrated by the unenviable experience of the North Carolina Moravians during the closing phase of the American Revolution. On one occasion an American colonel relieved the Salem settlement of 120 gallons of their brandy and likewise impressed one of their wagons for the

[76] Fitzpatrick, *Writings of George Washington*, 9:105.
[77] Ibid., 73–74.
[78] Ibid.
[79] James Alton James, ed., *George Rogers Clark Papers, 1771–1781,* Collections of the Illinois State Historical Library, 8, Virginia Series, 3 (Springfield, Ill., 1912): 101.

transportation.[80] On the same day (June 12, 1780) 25 additional gallons of brandy were taken from the Bethabara settlement by another American officer.[81] An additional horror of war was inflicted on the peace-loving Moravians when, shortly before the Battle of Guilford Court House in March, 1781, the Commissary of Lord Cornwallis appeared and relieved the Brethren of 100 gallons of the same product.[82] The British, however, considerately provided their own transportation for the impressed goods.

An indication of the magnitude of colonial distilling is provided by official action during the Revolution, as wartime conditions produced shortages of grain. In 1777 General Washington wrote that "some of the Southern States have already passed Acts prohibiting the distilling of unreasonable Quantities of Wheat and other Grain into Whisky, and I hope Pennsylvania will do the same."[83] Maryland might well have been one of the states to which the general referred. Bernard Steiner reports that its Committee of Observation provided heavy penalties in the case of "any miller who should grind wheat for distilling, or any distiller who should distil it, and these regulations were carefully enforced."[84]

In Virginia, concern over "the present alarming scarcity" and the "great quantity of grain consumed in the distilleries" led to an enactment in 1778 which prohibited the use of a wide variety of grains for distilling.[85] This listing, which included Indian corn, wheat, rye, oats, barley, buckwheat, both meal and flour, supplies additional proof of the expedient nature of colonial distilling—the distillers simply used whatever happened to be available at the time. Particularly pertinent to the present study is the fact that

[80] Fries, *Records of the Moravians*, 4:1545.

[81] Ibid., 1620.

[82] Ibid., 1742.

[83] Fitzpatrick, *Writings of George Washington*, 7:250. See also Cresswell, *Journal*, 180.

[84] Bernard C. Steiner, *Western Maryland in the Revolution*, Johns Hopkins University Studies in Historical and Political Science, 20, no. 1 (Baltimore, 1902): 31–32.

[85] Hening, *Statutes at Large*, 9:476. This enactment was in effect for only a three-month period—February 15 to May 1779.

the above restriction included Kentucky County, Virginia, which in all probability contained active distillers at the time.[86]

Wartime limitations on raw materials for liquor applied only to grain; brandy distilling continued to flourish, as did rum. The manufacture of rum was carried on in several states (exclusive of New England) both before and during the Revolution. In Charles Town, Maryland, a versatile coppersmith operated a distillery where, in 1753, he made and sold "Rum as good as any on the continent."[87] In nearby Baltimore, fifteen years later, the Purviance distillery suffered a temporary breakdown which made them unable to supply "half the home demands for rum."[88] A Norfolk, Virginia, rum distillery was owned by eight partners— of Tory inclination at an inauspicious period of history. This property was destroyed during the Revolution and, in a claim submitted to the British government shortly thereafter, was evaluated at approximately 4,284 pounds sterling.[89]

In somewhat over a century and a half, the seaboard colonies had become skilled in distilling and had accepted the use of spirits as a way of life. As the American frontier struggled across the mountains, Old World drinking customs were sometimes lost and often greatly modified amid the stresses of frontier life. The Great American Thirst, however, persisted.

[86] Ibid., 257–58. The effective lifetime of Kentucky County, Virginia, was December 31, 1776, to November 1, 1780.

[87] Kauffman, *Early American Copper*, 31.

[88] Letter of Samuel and Robert Purviance to Neil Jameison [*sic*], November 29, 1768, in Neil Jamieson Papers, Library of Congress, Washington, D.C., fol. 9, 2024. Cited hereafter as Jamieson Papers.

[89] Ibid., fol. 23, 5160.

2

Distillers Move
to Kentucky

T HE FIRST SETTLERS of the Kentucky country arrived
by one of the only two feasible routes. One of these routes,
and by far the more frequently traveled during the early phase
of settlement, was by way of the Wilderness Road which ran
from the vicinity of Long Island (Kingsport, Tennessee) to
Bean's Station and into central Kentucky by way of the Cumberland Gap. Access to the Wilderness Road was through Sapling
Grove (Bristol) to Long Island, or by way of Martin's Station in
the Powell Valley of southwestern Virginia. W. F. Dunaway
states that the overland route was used almost exclusively for
about ten years, with the river route becoming more popular
after 1785.[1] However, according to a contemporary observer, as
late as 1787 the Wilderness Road seems to have been the preferred means of access to the Kentucky country. In that year
Judge Harry Innes reported that "10000 Souls had been counted
to cross Clinch—about 2000 came down the River."[2]

The river route to Kentucky began at Redstone Fort in southwestern Pennsylvania, from which the emigrants embarked in
flatboats down the Monongahela River to Fort Pitt, thence by way
of the Ohio River to their Kentucky destination—usually Limestone (Maysville), the Falls of the Ohio (Louisville), or the

mouth of a stream providing access to the interior. A Kentuckian described his father's migration in the eighteenth century: "On the tenth day of October, 1782, he . . . sailed in [a] flat-bottomed boat, of which he was the owner, with five families of emigrants, from the Monongahela River, near the mouth of Redstone Creek, for the Falls of the Ohio River. At that time there were no persons residing on the Ohio, or near it, on either side from Wheeling to the Falls of the Ohio."[3] Some four years later George Washington referred to Redstone (seventy-five miles from Cumberland, Maryland) as "the general rendezvous for people going into the western country." The boats built there were "flat, very large and capable of carrying forty or fifty Tons: they cost from twenty to thirty pounds Pennsylvania currency, according to their size."[4]

Most of the people traveling these routes were from the frontier settlements of Virginia, Pennsylvania, North Carolina, and Maryland—probably in that order, with Virginia supplying the greatest percentage by far. Dunaway estimated that half of Kentucky's inhabitants at the time of statehood (1792) were from Virginia.[5] This is substantiated by other historians, in addition to contemporary travelers such as Gilbert Imlay and François André Michaux.[6]

[1] Wayland Fuller Dunaway, "Pennsylvania as an Early Distributing Center for Population," *Pennsylvania Magazine of History and Biography* 55 (1931): 158.

[2] Harry Innes to John Brown, December 7, 1787, Kentucky Historical Society, Frankfort, fol. 473. "Clinch" refers to the mountain between Bean Station and Cumberland Gap.

[3] Willard Rouse Jillson, ed., *Tales of the Dark and Bloody Ground: A Group of Fifteen Original Papers on the Early History of Kentucky* (Louisville, 1930), 91. Contains the autobiography of John Rowan. See also Gilbert Imlay, *A Topographical Description of the Western Territory of North America* (New York, 1793), 105.

[4] John C. Fitzpatrick, *The Writings of George Washington from the Original Manuscript Sources, 1745–1799* (Washington, D.C., 1931–1941), 29:136.

[5] Dunaway, "Pennsylvania," 159.

[6] William Henry Perrin, *History of Bourbon, Scott, Harrison, and Nicholas Counties, Kentucky* (Chicago, 1882), 83, 181; N. S. Shaler, *Kentucky, A Pioneer Commonwealth* (Boston, 1884), 23; Thomas D. Clark, *A His-*

Among these settlers were distillers such as William Calk of Prince William County, Virginia, who went to Kentucky in 1775, finally settling in present-day Montgomery County. The Calk family holdings, at the time of his departure, included a grist mill and a distillery.[7] On his way through the southwestern part of Virginia to the Wilderness Road he noted the following in his journal: "Wedn: 22d we Start early and git to foart Chissel [Fort Chiswell] whear we git Some good loaf Bread & good Whiskey."[8]

Colonel Evan Shelby, a distinguished frontiersman in his own right and father of Kentucky's first governor, moved his family from Maryland to the Holston country in 1771.[9] Settling on a large tract of land at Sapling Grove, the resourceful colonel operated Shelby's Station (a combination general store, tavern, and inn), engaged in land speculation, and operated a distillery.[10] Scattered pages from Shelby's account book reveal that some of the most prominent people of the day were among his customers. At various times in the year 1773 "Valentine Sarvayer" (Sevier), James Robertson, "Curnel Henderson," and "Daniall Boon" were indebted to the store-keeper for frontier necessities ranging from osnaburg cloth to loaf sugar. Of particular interest is an entry for January 26, 1773, which records Boone as having purchased, on credit, "2 Quarts of Rume" at three shillings each. Some indication of frontier mercantile practice is provided by an addi-

tory of Kentucky (Lexington, 1960), 75; Imlay, *Topographical Description*, 136; Reuben Gold Thwaites, *Early Western Travels, 1748–1846* (Cleveland, 1904–1907), 3:247.

[7] Lewis H. Kilpatrick, ed., "The Journal of William Calk, Kentucky Pioneer," *Mississippi Valley Historical Review* 7 (March 1921): 363.

[8] William Calk, Manuscript Journal, 1775 [p. 1].

[9] Oliver Taylor, *Historic Sullivan: A History of Sullivan County, Tennessee* (Bristol, 1909), 33.

[10] Archibald Henderson, "Isaac Shelby, Revolutionary Patriot and Border Hero," part 1, 1750–1780, *North Carolina Booklet* 16 (January 1917): 112; Betty Goff Cartwright and Lillian Johnson Gardiner, comps., *North Carolina Land Grants in Tennessee, 1778–1791* (Memphis, 1958), 8, 92, 108, 115.

tional entry which shows that Isaac Baker furnished 62½ gallons of rum to Evan Shelby at ten shillings per gallon, which allowed the modest resale profit of two shillings on the gallon.[11]

The first white men in the Kentucky country were hunters and surveying parties, and it is unlikely that they practiced any form of distilling on their hazardous journeys. Spirits were, however, an essential item in their supplies, and often in sufficient quantity to share with visitors. Cresswell noted his visit in June of 1775 to the camp of Captain Willis Lee (a surveyor) "who treated me very kindly with a dram of Whiskey."[12] With the establishment of permanent settlements such as Harrodsburg (1774), Boonesborough (1775), and St. Asaphs (1775), distilling soon became an accepted part of the Kentucky scene. Early records of these communities, also reflecting the immediate backgrounds of the people involved, tend to establish the practice of distilling well before the dates customarily assigned.

The idea of "the first distiller" has bemused Kentucky historians and writers for well over a century. Reuben Durrett credits Evan Williams of Louisville with the distinction (1783); others faithfully perpetuate this probable misconception by referring to the same source.[13] A few writers and historians are even wider of the mark—one designates as the first distiller Elijah Craig, who didn't arrive in the area until 1786; another maintains that "the first still in Kentucky had been set up in 1789."[14] This procedure,

[11] All ledger account information from Lyman C. Draper Manuscripts, State Historical Society of Wisconsin, 4 C 75, 11 DD 31–38. Isaac Baker was a close associate of Evan Shelby, emigrating to Sapling Grove with him. The latter's famous son was a namesake of Baker. See Henderson, "Isaac Shelby," 112.

[12] Nicholas Cresswell, *The Journal of Nicholas Cresswell, 1774–1777* (London, 1925), 85. This was the site of future Leestown, one mile below Frankfort on the Kentucky River, the first spot settled by whites in Franklin County; see Richard H. Collins, *History of Kentucky* (Covington, 1874), 2:242, 367.

[13] Reuben Thomas Durrett, *The Centenary of Kentucky*, Filson Club Publications, no. 7 (Louisville, 1892), 79; see also J. Stoddard Johnston, ed., *Memorial History of Louisville from Its First Settlement to the Year 1896* (Chicago, 1896), 1:55, 261.

[14] Harold J. Grossman, *Grossman's Guide to Wines, Spirits, and Beers*

at best, relegates to limbo an eight-year period of time (1775–1783) during which the settlers had done absolutely everything necessary, with regard to both facilities and materials, to be actively engaged in the production of spirituous liquors.

As a matter of fact, any argument as to the identity of Kentucky's first distiller should be considered purely academic. What actually happened was that a people moved in who regarded liquor as a necessity of life. The distillation of liquor or brandy occupied the same place in their lives as did the making of soap, the grinding of grain in a rude hand mill, or the tanning of animal pelts; distilling equipment was as necessary as the grain cradle, the hand loom, or the candle mold. Hence, with a modicum of protection from his savage neighbors, a roof over his family's head, and a crop approaching maturity, the pioneer's immediate concern was the disposition of his crop, including the sale or distillation of any surplus.

The first grain crop was undeniably corn, followed closely by small grain; the first domestic fruits were apples and peaches. Richard Collins asserts that "the first corn raised in Kentucky was in 1774, by John Harman, in a field at the east end of Harrodsburg."[15] On the first day of June in 1775, Nicholas Cresswell reported that he "found some Corn in a Crib, a Gun and some Clothes," near Harwood's Landing on the Kentucky River.[16] The presence of the other items would suggest the possibility that the corn had perhaps been raised by white men in 1774. Several other accounts, somewhat more authoritative, tend to favor the following year for this agrarian landmark. Levi Todd, who went to Kentucky in 1776, reported "some little corn raised" at Harrodsburg in 1775, and in the following year, "a great deal

---

(New York, 1964), 249; R. E. Banta, *The Ohio* in *Rivers of America*, ed. Hervey Allen and Carl Carmer (New York, 1949), 197. For information on Elijah Craig, see James Grant Wilson and John Fiske, eds., *Appleton's Cyclopaedia of American Biography* (New York, 1888–1892), 1:766.

[15] Collins, *History of Kentucky*, 2:605.
[16] Cresswell, *Journal*, 81.

of corn was fall cribbed at the different fields where it was raised."¹⁷ A petition to the Virginia Assembly (1779) from the "Distressed Inhabitants of Boonsfort" referred to the original settlement of 1775 where "all of the men raised corn here the first year."¹⁸ William Calk was one of these, as his journal for May of that year indicates that he "went out in the morning & kild aturkey and come in & got Some on for my Breakfast and then went & Sot in to Clearing for Corn."¹⁹ John Floyd, whose company was at St. Asaphs, reported in May of 1775 that the number of inhabitants "on these waters" did not exceed three hundred, and "they have about 230 acres of corn growing."²⁰ The unusual emphasis on corn production was not long in bringing results, for by 1780 the settlers of Boonesborough were in a position to sell a part of their grain surplus.²¹

Not only corn but other grain crops were being raised during the first few years of settlement. It was recorded by John Cowan that wheat was reaped on July 14 and 15, 1777.²² Lewis Gray may have been referring to this occasion when he stated that "the first crop of wheat in Kentucky was raised in 1777 on a small patch near the walls of Harrodsburg."²³ All of this early, constantly expanding production of an assortment of grains would tend to obviate any further necessity for importation of seed; it would also make an increasingly greater variety of grains available for distillation.

The production of tree fruits also received early attention. A

¹⁷ Draper Manuscripts, 48 J 10–11.
¹⁸ James Rood Robertson, ed., *Petitions of the Early Inhabitants of Kentucky to the General Assembly of Virginia, 1769–1792*, Filson Club Publications, no. 27 (Louisville, 1914), 49.
¹⁹ Calk journal [p. 3]. The Calk company had come via Elk Garden, Virginia, where they "suplid our Selves with seed Corn & irish tators." Calk journal [p. 1].
²⁰ Draper Manuscripts, 17 CC 180–81.
²¹ George W. Ranck, *Boonesborough*, Filson Club Publications, no. 16 (Louisville, 1901), 113–14.
²² Draper Manuscripts, 4 CC 30.
²³ Lewis Cecil Gray, *History of Agriculture in the Southern United States to 1860* (New York, 1941), 2:868.

contemporary journal recounts that the McAfee company, in 1775, "returned to the country early in March, & cleared two acres . . . & planted apple seed as well as peach stones" in the Salt River area, in addition to raising corn in the vicinity of Boonesborough.[24] The five following years proved fruitful indeed, for by 1780 "their *peach trees* which they had planted in the Spring 1775, were loaded with fruit, & the apple trees were some of them too large to transplant, such had been their rapid growth."[25] Collins credits John Boyle with planting peach stones in the fall of 1775, about three miles south of present-day Richmond.[26]

From such evidence it seems clear that well before 1780 Kentuckians possessed a variety of grain and fruit suitable for distilling. Considering their background and their customs, there is little reason to doubt that they showed equal promptitude in providing the necessary equipment. Several accounts suggest the possibility that stills were among the belongings of early migrants to Kentucky. Levi Todd's account relates the happenings in 1775: "This fall a great part of the adventurers returned to the Settlements Some to bring out their families, Some for Farming utensils." He followed this with a report for 1776: "This year commenced with the return of those who had been here the preceding year . . . Some families by water and Some by Land."[27] The McAfee journal describes the return of others from the older settlements in May of 1776: "They packed the greater portion of their household property & farming utensils on horseback across the mountains to *Brown's Ferry* on New River, or at this time the Kanaway river, where they made canoes & put their property on board, which also included seeds of various kinds & provisions, also whiskey & spirits bottled up & placed in the middle of their barrels of corn flour & seeds."[28]

[24] Draper Manuscripts, 4 CC 20.
[25] Ibid., 4 CC 27.
[26] Collins, *History of Kentucky*, 1:513.
[27] Draper Manuscripts, 48 J 10.
[28] Ibid., 4 CC 22.

The generic term "farming utensils" which appears in both of the above accounts could, and probably did, include some form of crude distilling apparatus. However intriguing this possibility, the fact remains that distilling could quite possibly have been practiced with equipment other than the customary copper fixtures. Distilling in wooden vessels was practiced in early Virginia; in 1652 Colonel George Fletcher obtained exclusive rights to such a process.[29] The component parts for a makeshift distilling apparatus (other than wood) could be found in most pioneer homes. One of the crudest forms of distillation involved nothing more than an open kettle and a heavy piece of absorbent goods such as a blanket. In this process, grain or fruit mash was heated in the container and covered with the blanket. This served as a condenser and was periodically relieved of its alcoholic contents by wringing.

Although some colonial stills were of great size and weight, many were of a size compatible with wilderness travel, particularly travel on the rivers. A still of fifty-gallon capacity could quite feasibly be transported on horseback. A 1786 inventory of the estate of an early Kentucky resident, Hugh Shiell, lists a still of twenty-gallon capacity, and its value as six pounds.[30] Based on the going rates for still manufacture at the time—six to eight shillings per pound of copper or per gallon of capacity—this outfit could hardly have weighed over forty pounds, even allowing for 50 percent depreciation in value.[31] At least two copper stills,

[29] William Waller Hening, comp., *The Statutes at Large: being a Collection of all the Laws of Virginia, from the First Session of the Legislature, in the Year 1619* (Imprint varies, 1819–1823), 1:374.

[30] Lincoln County Will Book A, 127. The terms "fifty gallon" and "twenty gallon" simply refer to the mash capacity of the still. Some distillers of the late eighteenth century used about twenty-four gallons of water per bushel of grain. This would allow, for example, about two bushels of grain for the mash in a fifty-gallon still.

[31] For rates on copper still manufacture, see Harrold E. Gillingham, "Old Business Cards of Philadelphia," *Pennsylvania Magazine of History and Biography* 53 (1929):214; (Lexington) *Kentucky Gazette*, September 19, 1795, hereafter cited as *Gazette*.

with a capacity of forty gallons each, were brought to Kentucky on horseback prior to 1781.[32]

With the advent of local Kentucky newspapers, beginning in 1787, the availability of distilling equipment became fully apparent. One of the first issues of the Lexington *Kentucky Gazette* contained an announcement by Samuel Blair that he had for sale "a quantity of excellent stills of various sizes."[33] Somewhat illustrative of the prevailing barter system, P. Tardiveau announced from Danville a large quantity of dry goods in exchange for suitable items of barter, including "some stills between 60 and 80 gallons."[34] The ready availability of distilling equipment at this time was not limited to Kentucky, by any means, for the stores of East Tennessee also included "assortments of stills" among their inventories of frontier necessities.[35]

Early Kentuckians, considered as part of a frontier population movement, followed precisely the same domestic patterns as did those who settled in extreme southwest Virginia, or those who moved on into eastern Tennessee. They were all subject to the same allurement—free land—made possible by successive wars, Indian treaties, state cessions, and finally the largess of the federal government. Furthermore, they all attached the same importance to distilling and followed the same routine in establishing the business. With home consumption the initial consideration, the settlers made use of whatever was first available in fruit or grain. Later, with increasing variety and a progressive surplus of raw material, production tended to follow the dictates of market demands. During the phases of early settlement, specific liquors were not representative of definite localities.

Versatility in liquor production and usage was an established

[32] Draper Manuscripts, 9 J 34.
[33] *Gazette*, November 24, 1787.
[34] Ibid., December 22, 1787.
[35] William Flinn Rogers, "Life in East Tennessee Near End of Eighteenth Century," *East Tennessee Historical Society Publications* 1 (1929):37.

fact long before the first still was erected in Kentucky or the eastern Tennessee area. Rye whiskey, traditionally associated with Pennsylvania and Maryland, was found throughout the Virginia–North Carolina region. The making of brandy and corn whiskey was similarly widespread. The North Carolina Moravians, at various times from 1756 until their distillery burned in 1802, not only produced large quantities of brandy from both apples and peaches but also distilled considerable amounts of whiskey—rye in particular.[36] George Washington's recorded distillery operations cover a span of some twenty-five years before his death. At first he specialized in peach brandy, principally for home consumption by the family and slaves; later he produced whiskey on a large-scale commercial basis. The principal ingredients used in the latter operation were corn or rye and occasionally some wheat.[37]

The prevalence of rye whiskey in the Old Dominion is further illustrated by a southwest Virginia will of 1780. James Mason, the decedent, had appointed Daniel Bartan as executor of the estate, adding, "and the said Bartan having agreed to distill sixty bushels of Reye for which I have payed the rent of the still."[38] In the nearby Sapling Grove area Evan Shelby operated his station and distillery. In 1780 Shelby executed an agreement which reveals much about early distilling practices:

An agreement or Bargin made this 19th day of February in the Year one Thousand Seven Hundred and Eighty, by and Between Colonel Evan Shelby of the one Party and Peirice Wall Distiller Of the Other Witnessith that the said Colonel Evan Shelby is to Provide Rye Meal and Malt at his Distillery Logs for Fuel and Candles and to find the said Pierce Wall in Diet and Washing

[36] Adelaide L. Fries, ed., *Records of the Moravians in North Carolina, 1752–1822* (Raleigh, 1922–1954), 1:160; 3:1096; 4:1598, 1623, 1625, 1734, 1739, 1859; 5:2055; 6:2575, 2716.

[37] Paul Leland Haworth, *George Washington, Country Gentleman* (Indianapolis, 1925), 182; Douglas Southall Freeman, *George Washington* (New York, 1948–1957), 3:78, 116; Fitzpatrick, *Writings of George Washington*, 36:122, 140, 141, 159, 168, 172, 302; 37:131, 211, 212, 214, 389, 415.

[38] Washington County, Virginia, Will Book 1, 45.

And to allow the said Peirce Wall the Fifth part of all the Whiskey He the said Pierce Wall makes Which is to be Divided Weekly The said Peirce Wall for his Part does hereby Engage to Cut his Firewood make malt and two Gallons of Whiskey of Every Bushel of Rye Distilled by Him or more if the Rye will produce it in Witness to the above both Parties have Interchangably set their hands and Seals the day and Date above Written

Witness Present	Peirce Wall
Isaac Baker	Evan Shelby[39]

The colonel doubtless used this rye whiskey to furnish his wilderness-bound customers with one of their necessities of life. It is not known to what extent, if any, the future first governor of Kentucky participated in the operation of his father's distilling business. However, it is certain that he absorbed many of the principles, both technical and commercial, for on more than one occasion during his first term of office Governor Isaac Shelby negotiated rental agreements involving his own distillery in Kentucky.[40]

Available evidence indicates that another later-day Kentuckian was associated with the production of rye whiskey in his native state. Harry Innes, a young lawyer of Bedford County, Virginia, received a plaintive letter from a fellow citizen, explaining an unforeseen setback in production and requesting financial assistance in the matter:

Sir.

Forty Bushels of Rye was whate I received of Col? Callerway [Callaway] to be distilled by Harvest Laste for which he was to receive one gallon per bushele, The misfortune of burning aparte of the Rye in maulte together with the kiln on which ite was drying has prevented my stilling any since and therefore from complying with my promise to him— . . . as I have note the money

---

[39] Contract between Evan Shelby and Peirce Wall, February 19, 1780, Kentucky Historical Society, Frankfort, fol. 850.

[40] See chapter 5, below, pp. 96–97.

by me shall be much obliged if you'll apply . . . for £450 giving your rect which shall be good agt his bond to me. I am

(Signed) W Leftwich

3 Oct' 1780[41]

The colonel was probably James Callaway, for among the Innes Papers is a "memor. of whiskey purchased of Col° James Calloway" in the amount of £792.0.0 for 44 gallons.[42]

One practice continued in Kentucky was that of court-established tavern rates, which were prevalent in Virginia and other colonies. The listing of these rates shows clearly the diversity of liquor available, and the price differential reflects the distinction between spirits produced locally and those of distant origin. Westmoreland County in southwestern Pennsylvania established rates in 1773 for whiskey, continental rum, and West India rum, with the latter spirits priced some 50 percent higher than the others.[43] The same conditions obtained for the taverns and ordinaries of the eastern area of future Tennessee. Listings in 1780 included West India rum, rye whiskey, peach or apple brandy, and continental rum; the prices similarly reflected transportation charges, and the varieties indicated local demand.[44] Rye whiskey, being the cheaper, was undoubtedly made in the immediate area, with Colonel Evan Shelby perhaps supplying a significant amount.

The rating practice became traditional in Virginia at a very early date, beginning in 1645; hence, it is not surprising that it continued to flourish throughout the Virginia-influenced areas of

[41] W. Leftwich to Harry Innes, October 3, 1780, in Harry Innes Papers, Library of Congress, Washington, D.C., fol. 20, part 1, 48. Cited hereafter as Innes Papers.

[42] Memorandum by Innes, July 1780, Innes Papers, fol. 20, part 1, 51. James Callaway was also the father of Harry Innes's first wife. See Mary Denham Ackerly and Lula Eastman Jeter Parker, "Our Kin": The Genealogies of Some of the Early Families Who Made History in the Founding and Development of Bedford County, Virginia (Lynchburg, 1930), 296.

[43] Alexander S. Guffey, "The First Courts in Western Pennsylvania," Western Pennsylvania Historical Magazine 7 (July 1924):156.

[44] Maxine Matthews, "Old Inns of East Tennessee," East Tennessee Historical Society Publications 2 (1930):25.

settlement.[45] A considerable progression of Virginia counties, with each including (at the time) the future state of Kentucky, enacted regulatory measures that closely followed in this tradition. Proof of the extreme prevalence of spirituous liquors is evident in the timing of the enactments; in almost every case, one of the first acts of newly constituted local governments involved some form of regulation for the retailing of liquor. Thus Botetourt County, in the year of its creation (1770) established tavern rates for West India rum, continental rum, French brandy, peach brandy, apple brandy, and whiskey.[46] With the creation of Fincastle County in 1772, court-assigned rates for ordinary keepers covered "continant Rum," West India rum, peach or apple brandy, and whiskey—the latter rated only two-thirds as high as the other items of domestic manufacture and half as high as the Caribbean product.[47]

In the newly organized county of Washington (December 1776), a court convened on January 29, 1777, at Black's Fort (Abingdon). One of the initial acts of this body was to rate liquors "for the ensuing year as followeth Rum at 16/ per gallon Rye liquor at 8/ pr gallon Corn liquor at 4/ per gallon . . . and so in proportion for a greater or lesser quantity." [48] The revised rates of 1779 reflected additional influences on sales of distilled spirits. Both an emphasis on quality and the wartime inflation of currency are evident in the following: "good rum at [£] 4. per gal. . . . good rye liquor full proof at [£] 2.s per gallon peach brandy at [£] 3."[49] Washington County at this time was traversed by practically all of the settlers who followed a land route to Kentucky.

The creation of Kentucky County from the now-defunct Fin-

[45] See, for example, Hening, *Statutes at Large*, 1:229, 300; 10:145, 147.

[46] Botetourt County, Virginia, Order Book, part 1, 9. For organic act, see Hening, *Statutes at Large*, 8:395.

[47] Montgomery County, Virginia, Order Book 1, 33. For organic act, see Hening, *Statutes at Large*, 8:600.

[48] Washington County, Virginia, Minute Book 1, 5. For organic act, see Hening, *Statutes at Large*, 9:257–61.

[49] Washington County, Virginia, Minute Book 1, 49.

castle County took place in 1776.[50] Unfortunately for distilling history, no court records are available for this short-lived county, but it is safe to assume that entrenched habits of liquor usage suffered no drastic change.

In 1780 three separate counties—Fayette, Jefferson, and Lincoln—were carved out of the existing Virginia county of Kentucky.[51] In accordance with firmly established precedent, one of the first acts of the local units of government was the promulgation of regulatory measures for strong drink. As had been the case in Virginia, these legal restrictions provide ample identification of liquor types and their availability.

What is certainly the first recorded effort to inaugurate local government in future Jefferson County occurred in June of 1780. Fragmentary records from the Falls of the Ohio describe the event:

[Torn] inhabitants of Lewisville finding it necessary (as we are [torn] from the Court of Justice) to elect Magistrates to regulate the many Villany's and bring to Justice all offenders do oblige ourselves to stand to and abide by the determination of Thomas Helm, William Pope, William Oldham, Andrew Hynes Morias Hansburry & Benjamin Pope
Given under our hands this Ult June MDCCLXXX[52]

Ninety-three law-abiding citizens affixed their signatures to this article of government and almost two centuries later most of the names are still legible. Among those adherents of law and order are three of the most prominent of Kentucky's early distillers—Jacob Myers, Evan Williams, and Marsham Brashears.[53]

One of the matters requiring immediate attention was recorded as follows:

[50] Hening, *Statutes at Large*, 9:257–61.

[51] Ibid., 10:315.

[52] Draper Manuscripts, 50 J 45. This was exceedingly prompt (or extralegal) action, since Louisville was not officially incorporated until May 1780. See Hening, *Statutes at Large*, 10:293.

[53] Draper Manuscripts, 50 J 45. Marsham Brashears was also one of the original trustees of Louisville. See Hening, *Statutes at Large*, 10:293.

At a Court held for the *Burrough of Lewisville* on Wednesday the Seventh June 1780 at 7 O'Clock in the Evening . . . Orderd that no retailers of *Whisky* shall presume to take more than One hundred & Sixty Dollars p Gallon for the same That no person shall presume to retail Liquors or keep a house of entertainment untill they enter into Bond & Security for the true performance of their Duty agreeable to Act of Assembly in that case made & provided and the rates of Liquors as pointed out by this Court. That if it shou'd be found that any retailer has adulterated the liquors by him sold the same Retailer shall be liable to the fines assess'd by this Court.[54]

Action of this sort by a self-constituted body of citizens is not a product of rash impulse, nor does it originate in a vacuum. This resort to corrective procedure recalls the ever-present frontier dilemmas of nonfunctioning local law enforcement and remote sources of legal recourse. Quite aside from the conspicuous example of war-influenced liquor prices, it is evident that an abundant supply of liquor was available in the immediate vicinity of precorporate Louisville. The resulting measures of control reflect the traditional approach used in the older settlements.

The formation of Jefferson County on November 1, 1780, allowed the establishment of a county court. The boundaries of this administrative unit embraced an unusually large area until substantially reduced by the creation of Nelson County on January 1, 1785.[55] An extract from the Minute Books of the Jefferson County Court for April 4, 1781, reads as follows: "The Court doth set the following rates to be observed by ordinary keepers in this county, to wit: Whiskey at 15 dollars per half pint."[56] Considering the hazards of Ohio River transportation at the time, it is unlikely that importations by water could have constituted the entire supply of liquor for this large county.

Of additional significance is the fact that the court saw fit, at

[54] Draper Manuscripts, 50 J 46.
[55] Hening, *Statutes at Large,* 11:469–70.
[56] Draper Manuscripts, 51 J 104.

the same time, to "appoint the Station called Doudel's [Dowdall's] station at the ferry on Salt River, to be the place for holding courts in this county."[57] This would imply that the center of population for the county was some fifteen to twenty miles removed from the immediate area of Louisville, and that liquor supplies were either of local production or from the neighboring Harrodsburg area via the Salt River.

Further evidence of Kentucky-produced liquor appears in the court records of Lincoln County. Shortly over five months after the county was officially created, the court of April 18, 1781, promulgated the most informative list of rates yet issued anywhere in Kentucky. It was ordered that the price of liquor be regulated as follows:

For every Gallon of good Rum . . . . . 72..0..0
For every Gallon of good Brandy . . . . 80..0..0
For every Gallon of good Whiskey . . . . 72..0..0
For every Gallon of indifferent
  or bad Whiskey . . . . 24..0..0[58]

This strongly suggests that distillers were in business somewhere in the immediate surroundings. Frontier whiskey was probably bad enough, at best; it is quite unlikely that "indifferent or bad whiskey" would be subjected to the prohibitive freight rates occasioned by several hundred miles of wilderness travel. By the year 1784, the rated prices of liquor had dwindled and more nearly approximated prewar conditions. "Whiskey full proof" was rated at twelve shillings per gallon and "common whiskey" at ten.[59] Again, this quality distinction is highly suggestive of local production.

Collins offers a brief mention of "some distilleries built south of the Kentucky river for distilling spirits from Indian corn" for the year of 1783.[60] This would appear to be a sizeable understatement,

[57] Ibid.
[58] Lincoln County Order Book 1, 8.
[59] Ibid., 241.
[60] Collins, *History of Kentucky*, 1:20. See also Mann Butler, *A History of the Commonwealth of Kentucky* (Louisville, 1834), 142.

for there is simply too much evidence of distilling activity prior to his date. Either the early Kentuckians were producing their own liquor well before 1783, or else they had the most efficient system of importation and distribution known in the history of colonial America. Extant evidence, in one form or another, indicates that by 1783 liquor was available in all areas of settlement, particularly the counties of Lincoln and Jefferson.

Records of individual involvement in aspects of the liquor business, while not completely conclusive, are useful in identifying pioneers of the distilling industry. One man who has some claim (backed by recorded evidence) to being Kentucky's first distiller is Marsham Brashears. It will be recalled that he was a signatory to the article constituting "burrough" government for Louisville; he was also one of the original trustees named at the incorporating of Louisville. On a deed, proved and recorded May 7, 1782, Brashears purchased 660 acres of land from Benjamin Pope and James Patten. The consideration was "165 gallons of good merchantable Whiskey, this day delivered by Marsham Brashears."[61] As locally produced spirits were a universal medium of exchange on the frontier, this transaction strongly suggests that Brashears himself had manufactured the whiskey.

Another Kentuckian who may have been among the early distillers was Jacob Froman of Lincoln County. In the June term of 1782 he proved to the court's satisfaction that he had raised a crop of corn in 1776, thus being entitled to his settlement (400 acres) and a preemption of one thousand acres adjoining.[62] Froman was subsequently presented by the grand jury on two occasions (December 1784 and March 1785) for retailing liquor without

[61] Willard Rouse Jillson, ed., "Index of Minute Book A (1780–1783), Jefferson County Court, Virginia," *Register of the Kentucky Historical Society* 53 (January 1955):47.
[62] Lincoln County Order Book 1, 17. For contemporary information regarding preemption and settlement, see John Filson, *The Discovery, Settlement and Present State of Kentucke* (Wilmington, Del., 1784), 36–38. See also Humphrey Marshall, *History of Kentucky* (Frankfort, 1824), 1:85–87.

license.[63] Although his corn crop, being customary, is not necessarily indicative, such repeated sales suggest that Froman may have been retailing the product of his own still.

Bartlett Searcy "of Fiat [Fayette] County and State of Virginia" recorded his will in September 1784, in which he devised "to John my son a ninety six gallon Still and equippage." The designated executor for this instrument was "Cono! Daniel Boone," and his brother, Squire Boone, was one of the witnesses.[64] Searcy showed considerably more foresight than was customary in the eighteenth century; he was not on his deathbed when the will was drawn up. A recorded inventory of the Searcy estate in 1792 lists some items of "equippage," including "three marsh [mash] tubs," but the still had apparently been disposed of before his demise. The inventory also included "one bond for one hundred gallons of whiskey" on Jacob Myers, who, incidentally, represents one of the more logical claimants to the title of Kentucky's first distiller.[65]

In adjoining Lincoln County the will of Hugh Shiell, dated August 24, 1785, directed that his executrix "shall sell my stills and brewing utensils and as much of my lands, as besides the stills and brewing utensils may be necessary for that purpose for the payment of my just debts."[66] An inventory of this estate was taken the following February; it included three stills at 250 gallons capacity, valued at 106/5/0, and one 20-gallon still with a value of 6 pounds.[67] The four stills (with a combined capacity of 270 gallons of mash) and brewing utensils obviously represented a sizeable investment and were hardly current acquisitions at the time Shiell felt constrained to execute his will. He conceivably could have been engaged in distilling for several years.

The judicial District of Kentucky was formed in 1783; im-

[63] Kentucky District Court Order Book, 1783–1786, 49, 160–61.

[64] Woodford County Will Book A, 16–18. This will was executed while Woodford County was a part of Fayette County.

[65] Ibid., 62–68.

[66] Lincoln County Will Book A, 121–24. The relict of Hugh Shiell became the second wife of Judge Harry Innes and subsequently the mother-in-law of John J. Crittenden.

[67] Ibid., 127.

mediately after this, the first District Court opened at Harrodsburg on March 3.[68] One of the first acts of the grand jury was the presentment of nine individuals charged with retailing spirituous liquors without license.[69] Lending additional credence to the idea of pre-1783 distilling, this action identified persons from all three of the then-existing counties of Kentucky. Quite possibly some of the implicated retailers had been charged with their offenses for some time before the establishment of this judicial district—certainly 1782, at the least.

The presentments of the "Grand Jury of Inquest" at the May 1783 term of the Lincoln County Court also listed nine persons charged with retailing spirits without a license. Included in this group were one woman (perhaps Kentucky's first female distiller) with two offenses, and a man with five separate counts against him.[70] Interestingly enough, the named informant in the woman's case bears the same name as a distiller who, some ten years later, was brought before the Federal Court for failing to conform to the excise law.[71] Another of the nine suspects apparently realized "the error of his ways" for, at the June term of court in 1784, he applied for and received license to "keep an ordinary" during one year at Whitley's Station.[72]

By 1784 the population of Kentucky was estimated to be "upwards of thirty thousand souls."[73] Frontiersmen accustomed to the use of distilled products had accomplished this settlement in an area where raw materials for distillation grew well. It is most likely that liquor was one of their earliest farm products.

[68] Collins, *History of Kentucky*, 1:20. Kentucky District Court Order Book, 1783–1786.
[69] Kentucky District Court Order Book, 1783–1786, 8–10. Included in this group was the founder of Harrodsburg, James Harrod, and his brother William.
[70] Lincoln County Order Book 1, 47–48.
[71] Willard Rouse Jillson, *Early Kentucky Distillers, 1783–1800* (Louisville, 1940), 44.
[72] Lincoln County Order Book 1, 180. Whitley's Station was two miles southwest of Crab Orchard. Groups congregated in this area for return trips to the older settlements. See Collins, *History of Kentucky*, 2:22.
[73] Filson, *Discovery, Settlement*, 28–29.

3

The Product Improves

FOR THE SAKE of sentiment and romantic tradition, it would be pleasant to record that a full-blown bourbon whiskey industry emerged from the limestone-layered soil of Kentucky at this time. However, the facts do not bear this out. The evidence suggests that, despite the taste of the early settlers for spirits, there was no such institution as a distinctive frontier beverage. The first few years of settlement were conspicuous for the introduction and use of a considerable variety of fruit and of grains other than the indigenous Indian corn. Accordingly, the distiller discriminated little in his choice of raw material and there was a corresponding lack of bias on the part of the consumer.

In the interest of historical precision it is unfortunate that most of the early references to distilled products (grain-based) tend to use all-inclusive terms—whiskey, spirits, liquor, and the like—thus leaving unanswered the question of exact grain content. This is equally true in the case of court actions and newspaper advertisements. For example, a quite early notice by John Bradford, the first editor of the Lexington *Gazette*, informed his readers that he would receive subscription payments in whiskey, among other items of country produce.[1] Many further examples of this practice appeared in the *Gazette*, continuing well past the turn of the century. A Fayette County landowner, Benjamin Carruthers, inserted a notice in 1790 which referred to his bond for 327 gallons of merchantable liquor, used as payment in a land purchase.[2] Following the enactment of a federal excise tax in 1791, the newly appointed Inspector of Revenue for the Kentucky District of Virginia, Thomas Marshall, promptly made use of the press to serve notice on distillers of spirits.[3] In similar vein, sporadic advertisements featured distilled spirits, good old spirits, and spirituous liquors, with no further indication of the precise grain components. Typical of this exercise in generalities was a listing of exports from Louisville for the first six months of 1802; it included spirits distilled of domestic produce.[4]

Several factors favored an emphasis on corn production and the use of any surplus in distilling. To begin with, corn was an indigenous grain; it provided an ideal, perhaps the best, initial crop for newly cleared land; it furnished food for both the settlers and their animals; it yielded considerably more per acre than did the smaller grains; and finally, with the possible exception of rye, corn mash offered an unmatched output of distilled spirits. For these reasons and regardless of vague product descriptions, corn was a significant factor in whiskey production from the onset of permanent settlement in Kentucky.[5]

There are in existence a few records which identify corn as the principal ingredient used by some pioneers in the Kentucky dis-

---

[1] *Gazette*, November 22, 1788.

[2] Ibid., December 8, 1790.

[3] Ibid., June 18, 1791.

[4] Ibid., March 29, 1794; April 15, May 6, 1797; August 6, 1802.

[5] For Kentucky grain production, see: John Filson, *The Discovery, Settlement and Present State of Kentucke* (Wilmington, Del., 1784), 24–25; Harry Toulmin, *A Description of Kentucky, in North America* (London, 1792), 84; Gilbert Imlay, *A Topographical Description of the Western Territory of North America* (New York, 1793), 101, 134; Thomas Cooper, *Some Information Respecting America* (London, 1794), 35; Thomas Ashe, *Travels in America, Performed in 1806* (London, 1808), 240; Reuben Gold Thwaites, ed., *Early Western Travels, 1748–1846* (Cleveland, 1904–1907), 4:197. For still output, see: Cooper, 122; Henry Wansey, *An Excursion to the United States of North America, in the Summer of 1794* (Salisbury, England, 1798), 164; Michael August Krafft, *The American Distiller* (Philadelphia, 1804), 88–95; Anthony Boucherie, *The Art of Making Whiskey* (Lexington, Ky., 1819), 10; Harrison Hall, *The Distiller* (Philadelphia, 1818), 142–46.

tilling industry. In March of 1789, Elijah Craig (the oft-reputed originator of bourbon whiskey) informed his legal representative, Judge Harry Innes, that a man from Pennsylvania was "Coming to make Corn, [and] I suppose will be hear soon."[6] It is entirely possible that Reverend Craig was referring to a crop of corn, but considering the distance involved, it is more likely that the anticipated visitor was coming to distill corn liquor. Gilbert Imlay (c. 1792) remarked on "spirits distilled from corn" as constituting one of the "ordinary beverage[s] of the country."[7] The diary of a future Union County resident, Captain Jonathan Taylor, contains detailed instructions for making corn whiskey, both with and without the addition of rye.[8] Although the recipe is undated, much of the diary was written at the time of General Anthony Wayne's campaign at Fallen Timbers and the treaty negotiations at Greenville, in 1794 and 1795 respectively. This would indicate that the recipe was in use before the turn of the century.

A work published in Lexington, Kentucky, in the early nineteenth century, containing reasonably complete coverage of the subject, enumerated the principal ingredients of whiskey at the time: "Whiskey is made either with rye, barley, or Indian corn. One, or all those kinds of grains is used, as they are more or less abundant in the country. I do not know how far they are mixed in Kentucky; but Indian corn is here in general the basis of whiskey, and more often employed alone."[9] However, to judge from the early and extensive publicity that rye whiskey received in Kentucky, it appears to have caught up with corn whiskey in the early laps of the popularity race, perhaps even outstripping it. The early popularity of rye and its corresponding extensive production are explained in part by William Henry Perrin: it constituted pasturage for stock in the winter and early spring; it could then become a grain crop, used to feed hogs for the early market; and, if not used

[6] Craig to Innes, March 5, 1789, Innes Papers, fol. 20, part 2, 211.

[7] Imlay, *Topographical Description*, 139.

[8] Jonathan Taylor, Manuscript Diary, 1774–1815 (?), Filson Club, Louisville, Kentucky.

[9] Boucherie, *Art of Making Whiskey*, 9–10.

thus, could be harvested and converted into whiskey.[10] Perrin might have included its usefulness as a cover crop for any recently cultivated land; to a small extent, soil conservation was being practiced by some Americans even then.[11] However, because of their Virginia-Pennsylvania background, some of the settlers may well have planted rye with the idea of whiskey production primarily in mind.

Contributing to the expanded production of rye and other small grain was a strain in international relations which resulted in a lengthy closing of West Indian ports to American shipping toward the end of the eighteenth century. Gray noted the "various obstructions to West Indian trade" and a "wide-spread tendency to substitute cereal beverages for rum."[12] In 1794 Tench Coxe estimated that over 100 distilleries would be affected by the drastic reduction in their supply of molasses, that importation of distilled spirits from Britain had decreased by over one million gallons, and that two million bushels of grain were currently required for the four million gallons of distilled spirits annually consumed in the United States.[13] Adam Seybert's figures showed that the importation of molasses for 1800 had dwindled to about 66 percent of what it had been in 1790. The distillation of rum showed an even greater decrease for the same years, with only 42 percent of the 1790 total being produced at the turn of the century.[14]

Travelers in the early nineteenth century noted the widespread use of rye in Kentucky whiskey production. Michaux, commenting on small-grain production in 1802, observed that "rye and oats come up also extremely well in Kentucky. The rye is nearly all

[10] William Henry Perrin, *History of Bourbon, Scott, Harrison, and Nicholas Counties, Kentucky* (Chicago, 1882), 63.

[11] John C. Fitzpatrick, ed., *The Diaries of George Washington, 1748–1799* (Boston, 1925), 1:185–87.

[12] Lewis Cecil Gray, *History of Agriculture in the Southern United States to 1860* (New York, 1941), 2:609. See also Victor S. Clark, *History of Manufactures in the United States* (New York, 1929), 1:230.

[13] Tench Coxe, *A View of the United States of America* (Philadelphia, 1794), 107, 227.

[14] Adam Seybert, *Statistical Annals* (Philadelphia, 1818), 261.

made use of in the distilling of whiskey."[15] Fortesque Cuming related his encounter with a floating store during a voyage down the Ohio River in 1807. He observed that several copper stills constituted a part of the merchandise and attributed this to the prevailing use of such wares "throughout the whole western country for distilling peach and apple brandy, and rye whiskey."[16] Not a word concerning corn whiskey in either of these travel accounts!

References to rye whiskey are abundant in the newspaper advertisements of the time. In 1796 a Lexington firm wanted to hire "a good DISTILLER: one who can come well recommended for his knowledge of the business, his honesty and industry, . . . the highest price will be given . . . for good clean RYE."[17] In nearby Scott County, Cary Clarke advised the public in 1812 that "I will give two shillings and 3 pence per bushel in cash, for Rye, delivered at my distillery in Georgetown."[18] Two years later, a Louisville grocery store was featuring "Rum, French Brandy, Old Rye Whiskey, common rye whiskey, Apple and Peach Brandy," in its current stock of liquors.[19] In view of this demonstrable popularity of rye whiskey, writers of a later day have been somewhat remiss in referring almost solely to corn distillates (including bourbon) for the early period.

In much the same fashion, the scope and magnitude of brandy distilling have been almost completely and inexplicably ignored in twentieth-century accounts. Various earlier accounts, however, testify to the prevalence of both apple and peach orchards from New England to the Louisiana area.[20] If any single domestically distilled product of the entire eighteenth century had been selected

---

[15] Thwaites, *Early Western Travels*, 3:240.

[16] Ibid., 4:116.

[17] *Gazette*, October 8, 1796.

[18] *Georgetown Telegraph*, January 30, 1812. Cited hereafter as *Telegraph*.

[19] *Louisville Correspondent*, September 21, 1814. Cited hereafter as *Correspondent*.

[20] Harry J. Carman, ed., *American Husbandry*, Columbia University Studies in the History of American Agriculture, no. 6 (New York, 1939), 41; Thwaites, *Early Western Travels*, 3:256, 269.

for its universality and premium qualities, it would have been a fruit distillate—probably peach brandy. Many writings recognized the supposedly superior qualities of this beverage. In 1786 George Washington apologized to his friend, the Marquis de LaFayette, for being unable to include "an anchor of old peach brandy" with a barrel of Virginia hams which Mrs. Washington was sending to Madame de LaFayette.[21] Tench Coxe waxed eloquent concerning "the exquisite brandy [which] is distilled from the extensive peach orchards, . . . and may be made in the greater part of our country."[22] Colonel Jeremiah Wadsworth, a Representative from Connecticut, valued good peach brandy to the extent that he enlisted the assistance of a fellow congressman, James Madison, in locating "a Barrel or half Barrel of the best Peach Brandy." Madison's letter to his father, reporting the colonel's wishes, included detailed instructions for quality, age, and the type of container.[23]

Michaux was impressed with the numerous peach trees in Kentucky and the disposal of the crop: "The immense quantity of peaches which they gather are converted in brandy, of which there is a great consumption in the country, and the rest is exported. A few only of the inhabitants have stills; the others carry their peaches to them, and bring back a quantity of brandy proportionate to the number of peaches they carried, except a part that is left for the expense of distilling. Peach brandy sells for a dollar a gallon, which is equal to four English quarts."[24] The practice of still hire had a long tradition and helps to account for the widespread use of brandy and other products of the still.[25] The relatively sizeable in-

[21] John C. Fitzpatrick, *The Writings of George Washington from the Original Manuscript Sources, 1745–1799* (Washington, D.C., 1931–1941), 28:457. An "anchor" would have been about ten gallons.

[22] Coxe, *View of the United States*, 92.

[23] Gaillard Hunt, ed., *The Writings of James Madison* (New York, 1900–1910), 6:105.

[24] Thwaites, *Early Western Travels*, 3:242.

[25] Stevenson Whitcomb Fletcher, *Pennsylvania Agriculture and Country Life, 1640–1840* (Harrisburg, 1950), 1:290; Jack P. Greene, *The Diary of Colonel Landon Carter of Sabine Hall, 1752–1778* (Charlottesville, 1965), 1:510, 770.

vestment occasioned by still ownership was quite often completely beyond the means of small farmers.

As additional counties were created in Kentucky, the court-established tavern rates continued to list brandy as a tavern commodity. Bourbon County came into being on the first of May 1786, and a court convened in the following month. The first pronouncements of this court included tavern rates for whiskey and brandy. The same items were again rated in 1787, and in 1788 were even more specifically categorized as peach brandy, apple brandy, and whiskey.[26] Mason County was established on May 1, 1789, and twenty days later the court established rates for a variety of liquors, including whiskey and apple and peach brandy.[27] The April 1790 court for Woodford County (established in 1789) included the same listings for their initial rating of spirits.[28]

Many newspaper advertisements featuring brandy reflected the statewide presence of this commodity in appreciable quantities. In 1793 the Lexington weekly contained a notice from Mercer County wherein "five hundred gallons of Peach Brandy" were offered for sale.[29] In 1796 a notice of land for sale in the Hanging Fork area contained the following suggestive description: "On it is a peach orchard of six hundred trees, that has made four hundred gallons of brandy in one year, and every appearance of there being sufi-cient [sic] fruit to make five hundred this season; with an apple orchard of four hundred flourishing trees."[30]

[26] Bourbon County Order Book, 1786–1789, 10, 70, 147. For creation of Bourbon County, see William Waller Hening, comp., *The Statutes at Large: being a Collection of all the Laws of Virginia, from the First Session of the Legislature, in the Year 1619* (Imprint varies, 1819–1823), 12:89–90.

[27] Mason County Order Book A, 5.

[28] Woodford County Order Book A, 89–90. For creation of Mason and Woodford counties, see Hening, *Statutes at Large*, 12:658, 663–64, respectively. At the time of its creation, Woodford County included present-day Scott County; the latter is often erroneously referred to as having once comprised a part of Bourbon County. See, for example, Harold J. Grossman, *Grossman's Guide to Wines, Spirits, and Beers* (New York, 1964), 246.

[29] *Gazette*, September 28, 1793.   [30] Ibid., July 2, 1796.

In nearby Bourbon County an early distiller, Laban Shipp, offered his farm of 500 acres for sale. Among the enumerated inducements to prospective buyers were "Between 4 and 5 hundred choice apple trees, and about four hundred bearing peach trees, . . . a good still house, with two good stills, one containing 118 and the other 96 gallons, thirty mash tubs &c. a tolerable good water grist mill on the same—a good new spring house, and two never failing springs."[31] This description was representative of sizeable operations of the period in that it included the adequate, year-round supply of water. In addition, and for obvious reasons, it was customary to locate a grist mill adjacent to the distillery, or vice versa. Quite often, in the presence of exceptionally bold springs and a sufficient fall, other water-powered operations were conducted—for example, fulling mills and saw mills.[32]

One such large-scale operation, involving both whiskey and brandy, was that of General Green Clay of Madison County, who was also the father of a future ambassador to Russia. At various times he saw fit to offer considerable quantities of his distilled products for sale. A representative advertisement appeared in December of 1800 in which he included 1,000 gallons of whiskey and 500 gallons of peach brandy.[33]

To judge from public records, Kentuckians were producing a surprising amount of peach brandy, along with their favored whiskey. From January to May of 1801, for example, the recorded export through the customs house for the Port of Louisville included 42,562 gallons of whiskey and 6,157 gallons of peach brandy.[34] Prices current, quoted from Natchez and New Orleans, reflect the popularity of peach brandy and the esteem in which it was held. From September 1800 to April 1802, whiskey quotations were from sixty-two to seventy-five cents per gallon. During

[31] Ibid., June 27, 1799.
[32] See, for example, discussion of Elijah Craig's establishment (p. 53, below).
[33] *Gazette*, December 1, 1800.
[34] Quoted in ibid., May 18, 1801.

the same period peach brandy price quotations ranged from one dollar to one dollar and fifteen cents per gallon.[35]

The presence of significant quantities of brandy in Kentucky at this time implied a corresponding amount of activity in the culture of fruit trees. As has been noted, peach and apple culture was practically concurrent with the first settlements. Initially, this practice involved the simple operation of planting the respective seeds, but it was not long before nursery-grown trees were available in sizeable numbers. Well before the turn of the century, a subscriber at Point Pleasant on the Ohio River notified prospective customers that he had for sale "fruit trees of almost every different kind."[36] In the following year (1795) a small plantation in the immediate vicinity of Cincinnati was offered for sale. It contained a "very thriving nursery, consisting of near six thousand trees, composed chiefly of Apple and Peach trees."[37] In the Bluegrass area in 1799, a considerable quantity of apple trees was offered for sale. Some two to three thousand trees, containing over fifteen varieties, were priced at one shilling each "if taken in rows"; otherwise the quoted price was 1/6.[38] It is perfectly true that home orchards comprised a part of the customary improvements on most farms, small or large. However, there was sufficient large-scale activity in fruit production, conjoined with distilling operations, to indicate that brandy manufacture was the primary intent.

Accounts of early Kentucky distilling fail also to mention the popularity of locally manufactured gin, cordials, and other compounded spirits. These, while never produced so voluminously as whiskey or brandy, became available in the final decade of the

[35] See ibid., September 1, November 10, 1800; February 16, April 27, October 5, 1801; April 9, September 24, 1802. Since distilled spirits were routinely accepted in exchange for merchandise, the advertisements of Kentucky stores occasionally reflected the acceptability and premium prices which characterized peach brandy. See, for example, *Russellville Mirror*, December 1, 1807, hereafter cited as *Mirror*.

[36] *Cincinnati Centinel of the North-Western Territory*, February 1, 1794. Hereafter cited as *Centinel*.

[37] Ibid., October 24, 1795.

[38] *Gazette*, August 15, 1799.

eighteenth century. Lord Sheffield had predicted in 1784 that the heretofore imported gin "may soon be made in America."[39] His prediction was soon borne out in the Kentucky area, for by 1795 "a quantity of old ginn, cordial, and whiskey of an excellent quality" was advertised for sale in the Cincinnati press.[40] In the following year another merchant of the same city listed an even more imposing selection of liquors: "Peach brandy, Apple brandy, cherry bounce, cordial, Ginn and cider."[41]

Supplies for this type of distilling were quite often provided by the frontier pharmacists of the day. Andrew M'Calla's Apothecary Shop in Lexington afforded a good example. His notice in the *Gazette* advised the public that he carried wholesale "the following articles for making French Brandy, Gin & Cordials."[42] There followed a comprehensive enumeration of exotic materials which significantly included 300 pounds of Holland juniper berries, the essential flavoring ingredient of gin. As an added fillip to those "who may incline to carry on the business of rectifying spirituous liquors [i.e., purification by redistilling] and the manufacturing cordials in an extensive manner," M'Calla offered to supply "genuine instructions gratis" with each purchase of material.[43] M'Calla included in the listing of merchandise "an exceeding good Copper Still, almost a quarter of an inch thick, containing better than 300 gallons, with a worm made of the very best pewter, having ten turns and weighing upwards of 500 lbs." This formidable outfit required seven hundred pounds of iron material for effecting its installation.[44] Many of the early apothecaries owned distilling equipment, though such apparatus was usually much smaller than the M'Calla still.

In 1816 the firm of T. Paxon and Company of Louisville notified distillers that 1,600 pounds of juniper berries were avail-

---

[39] Lord John Baker Holroyd Sheffield, *Observations on the Commerce of the American States* (London, 1784), 52.
[40] *Centinel*, September 5, 1795.
[41] Ibid., January 16, 1796.
[42] *Gazette*, March 29, 1797.
[43] Ibid; see also ibid., May 6, 1797.
[44] Ibid.

able for gin manufacture,[45] enough for at least six thousand gallons of full proof gin.[46] The choice of advertising terminology in a representative selection of newspapers—"prime country gin," "domestic gin," "American gin," "common gin"—also testifies to the regional aspect of this significant business.[47]

The relatively wide diversification of products was accompanied by significant developments in equipment during the first few decades of distilling in Kentucky. For a number of years Pennsylvania was a prime source for local distilling equipment, and it is probable that most of the stills laboriously hauled in by the first settlers originated in that state. Coppersmiths of the Quaker State achieved considerable renown for both the quality and the quantity of their distilling apparatus. One of them reportedly achieved a total output of 163 stills, a sizeable figure.[48] Perhaps the best known of the Pennsylvania coppersmiths, and certainly so in Kentucky, was Benjamin Harbeson of Philadelphia. Harbeson opened a Pittsburgh manufactory of stills in 1805. This fact was announced in Kentucky newspapers, together with the information that he would carry a constant supply of stills of all sizes and descriptions.[49]

One of the first local notices indicating the source of these valuable items of property was Robert Barr's Lexington advertisement in 1788. Included in the customary "fresh assortment of grocery and dye stuffs, just received" were "likewise two Philadel-

[45] *Correspondent*, January 15, 1816.
[46] Krafft, *American Distiller*, 161; *Gazette*, November 27, 1823.
[47] See, for example, *Gazette*, July 24, 1818; November 26, 1819; (Frankfort) *Argus of Western America*, September 30, 1829, hereafter cited as *Argus; Paris Western Citizen*, February 12, 1831, hereafter cited as *Western Citizen; Bardstown Herald*, December 22, 1832, hereafter cited as *Herald*.
[48] Henry J. Kauffman, *Early American Copper, Tin and Brass* (New York, 1950), 56. See also J. Leander Bishop, *A History of American Manufactures from 1608 to 1860* (Philadelphia, 1864), 1:574; Carl Bridenbaugh, *The Colonial Craftsman* (New York, 1950), 22.
[49] *Gazette*, July 23, 1805. For background on Harbeson, see Kauffman, *Early American Copper*, 37; Harrold Gillingham, "Old Business Cards of Philadelphia," *Pennsylvania Magazine of History and Biography* 53 (1929):214.

phia-made stills."[50] These products were apparently held in high
esteem by the Kentucky distillers for, over a quarter of a century
later, they were still being featured in the newspaper advertisements.[51] From Philadelphia this equipment was customarily con-
signed to Limestone (Maysville) by water and freighted overland
to its ultimate consignee; occasionally it was offered for sale at the
river landing. An advertisement in 1789 lists "a copper still, containing 120 gallons, with a good cap and pewter worm, for which
will be taken in payment, Cows and calves, ginsang or Furr skins;
the still is at Limestone."[52]

Local industry was not long in offering competition to the
Pennsylvanians, for several coppersmiths were operating in the
Kentucky environment well before the turn of the century. In
Lexington, Charles White respectfully informed the public that "he
intends carrying on the Copper Smith's business at this place, in
all its various branches, (to wit,) Stills, Brew and Die kettles
&c."[53] Some eleven miles southeast of Lexington, German Baxter
conducted coppersmithing at his plantation. In 1795 he offered
"For Sale, An Excellent, New-Finished STILL, containing 112
gallons—It may be had at the low rate of 7s. per gallon, if purchased before the 10th of September next, by applying to Mr.
Baxter, Copper-Smith, . . . Where the Still will remain till sold.
With said Still, A Brass Cock [faucet] may be had, with paying
the additonal sum of 30s.[54]

The coppersmith business was not confined to Fayette County,
by any means. Many members of the trade from other areas, lacking a local newspaper, made use of the Lexington press. At various
times firms from Bardstown, Danville, and Shelbyville advertised
their wares in the *Gazette.*[55] In localities where newspapers were
operating at the time, such as Louisville and Paris, occasional

[50] *Gazette,* January 5, 1788.
[51] Ibid., February 12, 1816.
[52] Ibid., June 27, 1789.
[53] Ibid., December 12, 1789.
[54] Ibid., May 9, September 19, 1795.
[55] Ibid., August 13, 1802; August 18, 1806.

notices of coppersmiths and their distillery equipment were likewise featured.[56]

The basic ingredient of still manufacture, sheet copper, was imported from Europe until after the American Revolution. This is evident in newspaper advertisements which featured sheet copper made in England and Holland.[57] However, by the end of the century, domestically rolled copper was undoubtedly being used in still manufacture. The most-quoted sources of this material were Baltimore and Philadelphia, but it probably originated with Paul Revere in Boston, since he was the only such manufacturer in the entire country as late as 1802.[58] A typical notice of the early nineteenth century is afforded by the Parker establishment's announcement that "copper in sheets & still patterns" had just been received from Philadelphia.[59]

Toward the close of the eighteenth century there was a noticeable trend away from small, family-type distilling. Distilleries increased in size and output, the manufacture of liquor became more sophisticated, and the distillers began to be specialized businessmen. There had actually been no such thing as an average distilling operation during the first few years of Kentucky's settlement. Still capacities had ranged from 40 to 120 gallons, with units occasionally deviating above or below this wide range. More often than not, the first stills were used singly, rather than in pairs. This is reflected in the many estate appraisals and inventories which enumerate but one still among the effects of the deceased distiller. A like situation is found in the personal notices of property for sale, which often included single units.[60] Few of the early frontiersmen could afford elaborate equipment.

[56] *Correspondent*, December 11, 1815; *Western Citizen*, November 25, 1817.

[57] (Philadelphia) *Pennsylvania Evening Herald*, May 4, August 6, 1785. Hereafter cited as *Evening Herald*.

[58] Bishop, *History of American Manufactures*, 2:96; *Gazette*, August 13, December 14, 1802.

[59] *Gazette*, July 17, 1804. Alex. Parker and Co. were located on Main Street in Lexington.

In the absence of a second still (or doubler) the distiller was confronted with a choice of two undesirable consequences. A single-run distillation resulted in an extremely unpalatable product. A second distillation—known then and now as doubling—consumed additional time. Well before the turn of the century, however, most of the distillers had accepted the idea of paired stills, with the smaller of the two representing the doubler. An advertiser in 1788, for example, served notice that he had "a likely young Negroe man" for sale; his desired price (in that age of barter) included "two copper stills one of about eighty gallons the other about forty gallons."[61] The definitive term "doubler" was being used in public notices a decade later. The Lexington firm of C. Beatty and Company offered "Three Stills of an excellent quality: two of which contain 120 gallons, each, and the doubler 60 gallons."[62]

Distilleries were often run in combination with other manufacturing—all served with water power from the same milldam. One of the earliest examples of this practice is furnished by a Baptist minister, Elijah Craig. At the Royal Spring, in present-day Georgetown, Kentucky, this versatile clergyman operated a paper mill, a rope walk, a fulling mill, and a distillery.[63] Fifteen miles from Lexington, at the mouth of Tate's Creek, there was an even more ambitious combination of manufactories. Included in the description of property for sale were a merchant mill and grist mill, a sawmill, a new hemp mill and rope walk, and a distillery with

---

[60] Woodford County Will Book A, 16–18; Lincoln County Will Book A, 172; Mercer County Will Book 1, 109–11; *Gazette*, April 26, 1788; June 27, 1789; June 30, 1792.

[61] *Gazette*, September 27, 1788. Additional information regarding paired stills may be obtained in court records. See, for example: Mason County Will Book A, 41, 359; Scott County Will Book A, 5; see also *Gazette*, November 7, 1798; March 5, 1802; *Georgetown Patriot*, July 13, 1816; hereafter cited as *Patriot*.

[62] *Gazette*, October 31, 1799.

[63] *Argus*, September 19, 1827; Richard H. Collins, *History of Kentucky* (Covington, 1874), 1:407, 516. The Royal Spring is today the water supply for Georgetown and the immediate surroundings.

"three stills containing about three hundred and seventy-five gallons."[64]

Many other counties—for example, Lincoln, Bourbon, and Madison—are represented in the Lexington press advertisements which featured amalgamations of this type.[65] The logical combination of distillery and grist mill was certainly the most common. An inherent advantage in such arrangements is obvious in the wording of a Harrison County notice inserted in the Georgetown *Patriot*: ". . . also a good never failing spring and spring house; together with a good distillery with two good stills, one 140 gallons and the other 92 gallons; also a sufficient quantity of marsh [*sic*] tubs, together with doubling kegs—a water mill sufficient to grind chop for the distillery and for the neighborhood."[66]

The approach of the nineteeth century witnessed other refinements in whiskey production. None had a greater impact on the infant industry than the application of steam. The use of steam in raising mash temperature to the vapor-point of alcohol obviated one of the worst problems heretofore encountered by distillers, a scorching of the mash through direct application of fire to the bottom of a pot-still. The possibilities for trouble were aptly described by a mid-eighteenth-century distiller: "The first accident which may happen by the fire, is when a distiller, by too great a heat, causes the ingredients to be burnt at the bottom of the still, by this means his liquor is spoiled by an empereumatic taste, and the tin is melted off from the alembic."[67]

Writing in 1794, Tench Coxe noted that "steam mills have not

[64] *Gazette*, January 23, 1796. The operator of an ordinary grist mill, so prevalent in early America, usually worked for a percentage (toll) of the grain brought in for grinding. In the case of merchant mills, the operator purchased the grain outright and stored it in his own granary for later processing according to market conditions. See Bridenbaugh, *Colonial Craftsman*, 19.

[65] Ibid., July 22, 1797; April 16, December 14, 1802; April 16, 1806.

[66] *Patriot*, November 2, 1816.

[67] A. Cooper, *The Complete Distiller* (London, 1757), 33; for a contemporary account of the prevalence of burnt whiskey characteristics, see H. M'Murtrie, *Sketches of Louisville and Its Environs* (Louisville, 1819), 129.

yet been adopted in America, but we shall probably see them after a short time in places, where there are few mill seats and in this and other great towns of the United States."[68] Within the next ten years, his prediction became fact. An early indicator of this innovation in Kentucky is to be found in newspaper advertisements which included boilers with distillery equipment. A notice of 1801 proclaimed: "For sale—by the subscriber, two COPPER STILLS, of a superior quality; one containing 125, the other 110 gallons. And also a COPPER BOILER, of 110."[69]

An advertisement of 1808, listing three European-made stills, alludes to the new process; it also provides an example of trends in productive capacity: "The two singling stills hold 165 gallons each—the bodies of either will weigh 500 gross. The doubler holds 75 gallons. They are large enough, with the addition of a boiler, to heat the beer to make 100 gallons of whiskey in 24 hours, if the new plan of distilling is pursued. They are strong made, with strait sides, to work fast on the European plan—with care, will last 100 years, and perhaps are the very best set of stills for their size, within the United States."[70] Considering the date of this notice and the relatively high output of whiskey claimed by the advertiser, the steam method was undoubtedly referred to. The same is true of the following distillery specifications from Lewis Sanders in Mercer County. It was described in the Lexington paper as con-

---

[68] Coxe, *View of the United States*, 39. Col. Alexander Anderson of Philadelphia claimed that he "discovered" the principle of conveying heat by steam and showed it to Mr. Jefferson in 1790. See U.S., *American State Papers, Finance*, 3:163. In 1794 there was a patent for a steam still, consisting of "one boiler which worked two stills." See Hall, *Distiller*, 52. This was probably Anderson's as he had a patent for a steam still on September 2, 1794. U.S., *American State Papers, Miscellaneous*, 1:423–31. Hall also says attempts were made in 1796 to evade the patent (including one case in Kentucky) "by forcing the steam through the wash [fermented mash], instead of letting it pass under a plate of copper, placed between the wash and the steam." See Hall, *Distiller*, 54.

[69] *Gazette*, March 16, 1801. For a number of years this suggestive, but inconclusive, wording was used in local press notices. See also ibid., November 27, 1801; March 29, 1803; February 28, 1807; *Correspondent*, February 6, 1815.

[70] *Gazette*, April 5, 1808.

taining "one heater 500 gallons, one boiler 500 gallons, 2 stills of 260 each—one of 160—caps, worms, tubbs, &c. with water sufficent to go into operation in the dryest time."[71]

The efficiency of the steam process, with either copper or wooden vessels, was recognized by the Congress in the wording of the Excise Act of 1813:

And for every boiler, however constructed, employed for the purpose of generating steam in those distilleries where wooden or other vessels are used instead of metal stills, and the action of steam is substituted to the immediate application of fire to the materials from which the spirituous liquors are distilled, for a license for the employment thereof, double the amount on each gallon of the capacity of the said boiler including the head thereof, which would be payable for the said license if granted for the same term and for the employment on the same materials of a still or stills to the contents of which, being the materials from whence the spirituous liquors are drawn, an immediate application of fire during the process of distillation is made.[72]

By 1815, irrefutable evidence testifies to the widespread use of the steam process in Kentucky distilleries and the advantages accruing therefrom. A farm on Floyd's Fork was advertised for sale on which there was "a Distillery worked by steam which can consume from twenty to thirty bushels of grain pr. day."[73] These production figures would convert to at least forty, and perhaps as much as ninety, gallons of whiskey per day at the customary yield. Serving to illustrate the trend toward high annual production, it was noted that "the Distillery is supported from two springs of never-failing water, which, will admit of the Distillery running the year through."[74] This would have enabled a possible yearly output of 25,000 gallons or more. In Fayette County in

---

[71] Ibid., October 9, 1810.

[72] U.S., *Statutes at Large*, 3:43.

[73] *Correspondent*, July 10, 1815. Two months earlier this newspaper had contained a notice that the "Louisville Iron Foundery" would make still boilers. *Correspondent*, May 8, 1815.

[74] Ibid.

1816 the Lexington Steam Mill was producing both flour and whiskey; the extent of its business can be judged from its advertised search for twenty to thirty journeyman coopers.[75]

Steam distilleries were active also in other areas of the state, and among them too there was evidence of greater efficiency in operation, with a correspondingly higher output. Six miles west of Russellville, in Logan County, "one of the finest stone distilleries in the State, of its magnitude," was offered for sale. "It is constructed upon the Steam plan and capable of making upwards of fifty gallons of whiskey per day, with the labour of two hands only."[76] An advertisement of real estate for sale in Harrison County in 1827, within one mile of Cynthiana, included "an extensive distillery, making from 50 to 60 gallons of whiskey per day."[77] Some twenty miles east of Louisville, in the following year, Smith Felps offered to sell his interest in "the Oldham Steam and Water Power Mills, Steam Distillery, Saw Mill, Store, and Blacksmith's Shop." This property included a "first rate Engine, calculated to run 4 pair of six feet stones: which, with the Saw Mill and Distillery, have undergone a thorough repair last season, and are now equal to new. The Distillery runs from 60 to 70 gallons per day."[78]

By far the largest and most ambitious project was the Hope Distillery in Louisville. This company was formed in New England, incorporated in Kentucky, and began construction of a large distillery in the summer of 1816.[79] It commenced operation in mid-1817, using a 45-h.p. steam engine and two English-made copper stills, which (together with the worms) weighed more than ten tons. The stills had a capacity of 1,500 gallons for the singling still and 750 for the doubler. The daily output of this enterprise was estimated to be 1,200 gallons per day in 1819.[80] However, in

---

[75] *Gazette*, July 1, 1816; see also July 19, 1817; February 27, 1818.
[76] Ibid., September 26, 1822.
[77] *Western Citizen*, May 19, 1827.
[78] *Argus*, May 14, 1828.
[79] *Correspondent*, February 24, March 29, 1817. Official date of incorporation was January 27, 1817; see William Littell, comp., *The Statute Law of Kentucky* (Frankfort, 1809–1819), 5:458.

1821, George Ogden reported that he "was informed, by one of the principal overseers, that this distillery produced fifteen hundred gallons per day."[81]

The contemporary advertisements of this concern left no doubt regarding its enormous potential, or the nature of its product. At the beginning of 1817 it was announced that "cash, and the highest market price will be given for any quantity of corn in ears, delivered at the Hope Distillery, Louisville."[82] By the end of the same month, a subsequent notice advertised for a large quantity of barley, rye, and corn for the ensuing season, adding that "the price to be fixed on at harvest, will be such as to induce an extensive cultivation of those grains, in a country, the soil and climate of which, are so well calculated to produce them."[83] An additional feature of the Hope Distillery was its planned utilization of the spent mash as a byproduct for feeding hogs. The annual output of pork to be derived from this venture was estimated at two to three million pounds. This procedure was widely used by distilleries of all sizes; various writers refer to it, before and after the turn of the century.[84]

More than any similar enterprise of the period, the Hope Distillery represented the trend which the industry was to follow. Nevertheless, this grandiose project ended as a business failure. Casseday reports merely that "this enormous establishment however did not realize the expectations of its proprietors and the project was abandoned. The buildings remained almost tenantless and useless for many years. They were finally burned."[85]

---

[80] *Correspondent*, March 29, 1817. For additional information on the Hope Distillery, see M'Murtrie, *Sketches of Louisville*, 127–31; Ben Casseday, *The History of Louisville from Its Earliest Settlement Till the Year 1852* (Louisville, 1852), 143.

[81] Thwaites, *Early Western Travels*, 19:40.

[82] *Correspondent*, January 6, 1817.

[83] Ibid., January 27, 1817.

[84] Ibid., March 29, 1817; M'Murtrie, *Sketches of Louisville*, 129–30; Thomas Cooper, *Information Respecting America*, 126; Krafft, *American Distiller*, 32; Boucherie, *Art of Making Whiskey*, 25.

[85] Casseday, *History of Louisville*, 143.

For a number of years, coincident with the use of steam in distilling, wood was used in various parts of still construction. The first recorded use of wooden construction in steam-type stills in Kentucky seems to have been in 1797. John Owings and Company opened the Bourbon Furnace and offered to supply "fifty gallon kettles . . . constructed in such a manner, that wooden tops may be fixed on them, so as to make them contain several hundred gallons. These kettles have been found in the distilleries where they have been used, to be as serviceable as an additional still."[86] In addition, wood was used in the construction of condensing chambers—between the still head and the worm. Judging by the extravagant claims for the performance of the new method, accompanied by glowing endorsements of distillers, there was considerable activity in this direction for more than two decades. The big selling points were economy of construction, reduction in labor, and a better-flavored product. A typical claim mentions the "improved plan of distilling spirituous liquors by means of steam through wood vessels without the trouble of doubling."[87]

It seems likely, however, that the experiments with wood in steam distilling were more in the nature of a fad than anything else. Although wood was cheap, it tended in time to become impregnated with mash and difficult to clean, with a resultant contamination of the product.

A far more lasting innovation that appeared at the same time was the use of copper condensing chambers. This process is completely described in a contemporary work on distilling by Anthony Boucherie. By using a series of three copper vessels ("urns") between the still head and the worm, Boucherie obtained "three successive rectifications [which] bring the spirit to a high

[86] *Gazette*, January 18, 1797. Writing in 1818, Hall discussed a considerable use of log stills in rural areas of Tennessee and Kentucky. These operated on the steam principle but for obvious reasons were never completely satisfactory. Hall, *Distiller*, 62–67.

[87] *Gazette*, October 15, 1811. See also ibid., May 21, 1802; September 20, 1803; October 2, 1818; *Argus*, April 25, 1827. In 1803, a patent was granted for an improvement involving the use of steam with wooden or other stills. U.S., *American State Papers, Miscellaneous*, 1:423–31.

degree of concentration."[88] His book of instructions explains a few of the inherent advantages: "The first is, that with a single fire, and a single workman, I distil and rectify the spirit three times, and bring it to the degree of alcohol; that is, to the greatest purity, and almost to the highest degree of concentration. . . . It lowers the cost of transportation, by two-thirds; because one gallon . . . represents three gallons at the usual degree. . . . [spirits] made with my apparatus, being at a very high degree, need no more rectifying, either for the retailer, the apothecary, or the painter."[89] This method was in keeping with a sound principle, for essentially the same type of still construction was being followed in the early twentieth century.[90]

The improvements in processing, particularly the use of steam, greatly enlarged the production of individually owned distilleries, and vastly increased the amount of available whiskey. To a somewhat lesser degree, this was true also of brandy and rectified spirits. Quantities of whiskey advertised for sale during the first two or three decades of the nineteenth century reached surprising totals. Several different areas of the state were represented in offerings, at various times, which ranged from several hundred to 8000 gallons.[91] Judging from the quantities that he listed in public notices, one of the largest operators of the day was General Green Clay of Madison County. On one occasion he featured 3,000 gallons of whiskey and four barrels of seven-year-old peach brandy. Some two years later the general's advertisement included "ten thousand gallons of Whiskey, Brandy, Cider, and Cider-Royal."[92] Following Clay's death in October 1826, a part of his estate was disposed of through a public sale; included in the inventory were "2 or 3000 gallons prime old whiskey, 1500 gallons old apple brandy, one steam and two copper distilleries."[93]

[88] Boucherie, *Art of Making Whiskey*, 28–31.
[89] Ibid., 36–37.
[90] John Fuller, *Art of Coppersmithing* (New York, 1911), 296–97.
[91] See, for example, *Gazette*, January 31, 1809; *Correspondent*, August 21, 1815.
[92] *Gazette*, April 4, 1807; January 17, 1809.

Such outputs were made possible by the constantly increasing yield of spirits per bushel of grain. Before the turn of the century, production had averaged one and a half to two gallons per bushel. By 1804, claims were being made for "three gallons of pure spirits, and sometimes more, from every bushel of assorted grain and malt that will be used."[94] In 1818, the patent stills were reputedly producing "$\frac{1}{10}$ to $\frac{1}{15}$ more liquor from any kind of beer, than either the old Copper Stills or the Steam Tub Stills."[95] A method of 1823 claimed that "three and a fourth gallons of good spirit have been made to the bushel of grain."[96]

All of the early-nineteenth-century trends toward increased production and specialization were highly suggestive for the future of Kentucky distilling. They were concurrent with rapid changes in the national scene. The direct use of whiskey as a medium of exchange had already undergone a significant reduction. The continually receding frontier had allowed the creation of successive states, thereby vastly expanding the marketing area. Expansion of transportation facilities permitted larger concentrations of distilled products and a corresponding improvement in distribution. The passing of the small-farmer distiller was not immediately at hand, but his chapter in the making of Kentucky history was written and finished.

---

[93] *Western Citizen*, November 15, 1828.
[94] *Gazette*, January 3, 1804.
[95] Ibid., October 2, 1818.
[96] Ibid., November 27, 1823.

4

As Useful as Money

A s w e h a v e s e e n, the pioneer Kentuckian was both a zealous distiller and a glad partaker of his own product. In this he followed precedent, and in this and other aspects of those liquorous days, we can observe strong parallels with the attitudes and customs of an earlier time.

We can reasonably assume, for example, that the builders of the frontier forts were inspired by, in addition to their fear of the Indians, occasional shots of hard liquor. In the spring of 1781, a new fort was constructed at a settlement which later became the town of Lexington. The expense account later submitted to the Commonwealth of Virginia listed, among other things, twenty-one quarts of "Liquor given to the men at sundry times."[1] Colonel John Todd's correspondence with the Governor of Virginia relative to this project mentions that "rewards in liquor to the men proved powerful incentives to industry."[2]

Liquor continued to be a useful medium of barter with the Indians. Thomas Baldwin's account of his captivity among the savages (1781) relates that his captors were "overtaken by another party of savages, twelve in number, on their return from Boonsboro, where they had been to exchange furs for whiskey."[3] Other accounts of the first few years of settlement confirm that the frontiersmen furnished liquor to the Indians, either through barter or otherwise. Kentucky's first historian, John Filson, reported from Post St. Vincent (Vincennes) in 1785 that "a number of

62

families was induced to emigrate thither these having Spirituous liquor with them found interest and a Support by trading in that article with the indians."[4] When, in the same year, Filson planned a trip to "Kentucke" he found "it was necessary to hire indian guides, which for a few bottles of Whiskey was soon procured."[5]

Any conference with Indian leaders was considered an appropriate occasion for generous distributions of liquor, and no one held this opinion in higher esteem than George Rogers Clark. His requirements for scheduled councils included "many gallons of taffia, whisky, or other strong drink."[6] In Filson's report on a council with the Piankashaw Indians at Post St. Vincent (1784), the reply of a chief to "My Great Father, the Long Knife" is quoted: "Some of your people mend our guns, and others tell us they can make rum of the corn. . . . we could never learn to make rum—God has made the White Flesh masters of the world; they make everything; and we all love rum—."[7]

The conciliation of Indians in the Old Northwest was not the only reason behind a continual demand for large quantities of spirits within that vast area. Even before the formal end of the Revolutionary War, military activity had increased to the extent that it was being reflected in a demand for extra supplies of liquor.

[1] James Alton James, ed., *George Rogers Clark Papers, 1771–1781,* Collections of the Illinois State Historical Library, 8, Virginia Series, 3 (Springfield, Ill., 1912):523. For act to establish the town of Lexington in 1782, see William Waller Hening, comp., *The Statutes at Large: being a Collection of all the Laws of Virginia, from the First Session of the Legislature, in the Year 1619* (Imprint varies, 1819–1823), 11:100–101.

[2] Quoted in Charles R. Staples, *The History of Pioneer Lexington (Kentucky), 1779–1806* (Lexington, 1939), 18.

[3] Thomas Baldwin, *Narrative of the Massacre* . . . (New York, 1836), 10.

[4] Quoted in Beverly W. Bond, Jr., ed., "Two Westward Journeys of John Filson, 1785," *Mississippi Valley Historical Review* 9 (March 1923): 327.

[5] Quoted in ibid., 329.

[6] James G. Randall, "George Rogers Clark's Service of Supply," *MVHR* 8 (December 1921):255.

[7] John Filson, *The Discovery, Settlement and Present State of Kentucke* (Wilmington, Del., 1784), 85–86.

Captain Robert George, commanding officer at Fort Jefferson, wrote to Colonel George Slaughter, commandant at the Falls: "In the Month of January [1781] I have the pleasure to inform you we were able to drink brandy, Taffia & Wine—with your good assistance Whisky too; but it has not made us so saucy, but we can drink all the Whisky you can send us. . . . I have the Pleasure to drink your Health in a bumper of your good Whisky."[8] This communication is strongly suggestive of Kentucky-made whiskey, as are many similar accounts.

In other respects, the demands of military logistics were a constant source of vexation, increased by wartime inflation and scarcity of reliable currency. Captain William Shannon, purchasing commissary for the Western Department, whose headquarters were in the vicinity of the Falls, described the situation in a letter to General George Rogers Clark: "I find it allmost impossible to purchase any thing without money." In the same message, however, he informed Clark that he had sent a boat to Post St. Vincent with three hundred gallons of whiskey about three weeks previously.[9] On one occasion Captain Shannon was involved in an official investigation concerning possible irregularities in the purchasing of supplies. The inquiry disclosed, among other things, that in 1780 one owner of whiskey had refused the inflated price of £45 per gallon for his wares; he would not accept the preferred bills on the Treasury of Virginia in payment.[10]

Both the preeminence of whiskey as a medium of exchange and the uncertainties of impressment are brought forth in a letter from Captain John Bailey to Colonel Slaughter. Bailey's missive, from "Post St. Vincence Aug: 6th 1781," included the information that "my Men have been 15 days upon half allowance, there is plenty of provisions here but no credit, I cannot press being the weakest party . . . if you have not provisions send whisky which will

---

[8] James, *George Rogers Clark Papers*, 507. "Fort Jefferson was located five miles below the mouth of the Ohio River at a spot called 'The Iron Banks' "; ibid., cxxiv.
[9] Ibid., 554.
[10] Ibid., 519.

answer as good an end."[11] This difficulty in the requisition of supplies was not experienced by General Clark's troops in their native habitat. For a number of years following the Northwest campaigns, claims were submitted for various amounts of whiskey which had been impressed in Kentucky for the use of Clark's men. For example, in 1797 Ezekial Howell wrote to Thomas Bodley of Lexington: "Another acct. I requested you to Endeavour to Settle was the amount of Ten Gallons of Spirrits that Coll. Robt. Todd press! when Gen! Clark went on that Ever Memorable Expedition against the Wabash Indians he has the Certificate & Can Give you better Information Respecting it than I Can."[12]

The Treaty of Paris yielded only an uneasy peace, and long thereafter the new country continued to experience threats and rebuffs in a predatory family of nations. Along the frontier there was fighting indeed—a ceaseless struggle to protect the new settlements from the forays of merciless savages. Thus it was that for almost four decades following the original settlements in Kentucky there were occasional mobilizations of considerable numbers of troops. These required vast quantities of liquor to supply the customary ration of "a gill of spirits to each officer and soldier in the state." Numerous enactments of the Virginia legislature established spirits as one of the components of "a ration of provisions," established price ceilings on spirits received by "all officers, sailors, and soldiers, raised by this state," and equated the militia with the continentals in determining eligibility for rations.[13] In addition to the usual allocation, extra rations were issued to working parties on special detail. John Armstrong, Captain Commandant at Fort Hamilton, reported to General James Wilkinson in 1792: "I have allowed the mowers one and a half rations

[11] Ibid., 581.
[12] Ezekial Howell to Thomas Bodley, August 25, 1797 (Kentucky Historical Society, Frankfort), fol. 460. This was by no means an isolated case; for similar actions on the part of the military, and the post-campaign demands for reimbursement, see Hundley to Innes, June 6, 1791, Innes Papers, fol. 20, part 2, 245. See also James, George Rogers Clark Papers, 4:247.
[13] Hening, Statutes at Large, 9:446; 10:19; 11:476–94.

per day, and both them and the hay-makers, half a pint of whiskey each."[14]

Following the inauguration of a central government, there was no significant departure from these practices. Federal legislation continued to define the liquor component of a "ration"; in 1790 this was specified as "half a gill of rum, brandy, or whisky," and in 1802 it was doubled.[15] An issue of the *Western Spy and Hamilton Gazette* for December 21, 1800, lured prospective recruits with the following advantages of army life: "an abundant supply of WHISKEY, FOOD AND CLOTHING of the best quality— TWELVE DOLLARS BOUNTY, and TEN DOLLARS per month, with comfortable quarters and a LIFE OF EASE."[16] An act of 1819 provided for fifteen cents and an extra gill of whiskey or spirits per day for noncommissioned personnel detailed to such work as building fortifications, surveys, and cutting roads.[17]

Kentucky was by no means the sole source of military whiskey, but obviously was well situated as a base of supply. This became even more evident as the expanding frontier brought into being new forts and military posts. Army purchasing agents customarily filled their whiskey quotas from several distillers; at times such purchases amounted to several thousand gallons per consignment. Major Thomas Bodley, acting in this capacity in 1813, received payment for "Four thousand six hundred & sixteen Gallons of Whisky purchased by him from sundry persons as per account rendered & delivered at Fort Amanda on the Au Glaize [*sic*] at one Dollar per Gallon, Contained in one hundred & thirty nine barrels."[18]

---

[14] Letter quoted in Charles Cist, *The Cincinnati Miscellany, or Antiquities of the West* (Cincinnati, 1845–1846), 2:15.

[15] U.S., *Statutes at Large*, 3:488.

[16] Quoted in Charles Cist, *Cincinnati in 1841: Its Early Annals and Future Prospects* (Cincinnati, 1841), 175.

[17] U.S., *Statutes at Large*, 3:488.

[18] Receipt, Thomas Bodley to John Piatt, Purchasing Commissary, May 1, 1813, Kentucky Historical Society, Frankfort, fol. 88. The Auglaize is a tributary of the Maumee River in northwestern Ohio. Fort Amanda was one of "three small forts [which] had been built to guard

Further indication of the sizeable quantities of whiskey involved in army purchases is the annual bid solicitations from the Commissary General of Subsistence. For well over three decades (1793–1827) the customary notifications to prospective purveyors of ration supplies were published in Kentucky newspapers. During the final ten years of this period detailed listings of destinations, and quantities of whiskey needed at each, were included. The aggregate of these requirements reached tremendous proportions; on one occasion it amounted to over 4,000 barrels, or in excess of 120,000 gallons of whiskey.[19] Because of its proximity to encampments and other military installations, Kentucky was a feasible source for nearly half of the total requirement.

Distilled spirits were considered of equal importance in many other phases of Kentucky life. In spite of Virginia's efforts at curtailment, the long-established tradition of treating continued in the Kentucky setting. In 1781 the candidates for burgess in Lincoln County were Benjamin Logan and Jacob Myers. It was later related by a contemporary that Myers (a distiller) "made free use of his whiskey, but the old Indian fighter distanced him & was easily elected."[20]

A notice in the Frankfort press (1808) is evidence that the practice of treating persisted after the turn of the century:

Fellow Citizens,

I have on hand a few barrels of good whiskey, which I had made to send down the river—but that Bargo law has discouraged me—and as I can have no sale for it in this country, I have concluded to become a Candidate to represent my county in the general Assembly: I think this the most honourable way to dispose of some property which might otherwise be of little use to me. I shall at all times, particularly between this and the election, be happy to see my friends at my house—I shall pay special attention

---

the supply route from Piqua to old Fort Defiance." See Alec R. Gilpin, *The War of 1812 in the Old Northwest* (East Lansing, Mich., 1958), 155.

[19] *Gazette*, August 20, 1819.

[20] Lyman C. Draper Manuscripts, State Historical Society of Wisconsin, 9 J 34.

to them during the election—and if elected implicitly obey their instructions.

I am fellow citizens with
Great consideration, your
Sincere friend,
John Grunter.[21]

This single-paragraph declaration of intent speaks volumes with respect to the conditions of the day. By implication, or otherwise, it is indicative of a wide range of frontier discontent: the remote market for disposal of agricultural commodities, the utter reliance on river transportation, the helpless susceptibility of the Kentuckians to the vagaries of international affairs for a quarter of a century, and the customary election practices of a frontier society. Alas for the whiskey-dowered political aspirations of Mr. Grunter, his name was not listed among the members of the legislature from Franklin County for the ensuing session.[22] It is not known whether this was a reflection on his character or on the quality of his liquor.

The historian George Ranck has described an instance of treating in nearby Lexington several years later, and some bizarre consequences:

It was then the custom for successful candidates at the close of the polls, to give a "big treat" to their constituents. On one of these occasions, Robert Wickliffe, Sr., "treated" to punch, a barrel of which was set in the middle of Limestone street, opposite the place now known as the Sayre Institute. A strong partisan on the other side, a somewhat notorious character, who was always after called "Dr." Napper, secretly dropped some tartar emetic in the punch. Such a scene as ensued beggars all description, and could hardly be limned with the pencil of a Hogarth. The retching and heaving, the sputtering, and spewing, and spouting, with
"The two and seventy stenches,
All well defined, and several stinks,"
Which assailed the olfactories of the passers-by was due notice

[21] *Argus*, May 26, 1808.
[22] Richard H. Collins, *History of Kentucky* (Covington, 1874), 2:241.

to give the participators in the debauch a wide berth. That was the last general political treat given in the interior of the state.[23]

In most instances, however, imbibing in early Kentucky took place under happier circumstances, and liquor was relished in all classes of society. Among the area's clergymen, regardless of denomination, the typical attitude toward distilling and moderate drinking was one of benevolent approval.[24] This, please recall, was some half a century before the tidal wave of Victorian righteousness engulfed the American plains.

Some of the first Baptist ministers in trans-Allegheny Virginia were prominent in the whiskey business, engaging in both production and distribution. The minister who achieved the most lasting fame in this respect was, of course, Elijah Craig of Georgetown. However, it is a matter of record that Elijah's brother Lewis, also a Baptist minister, dealt in considerable quantities of whiskey. One of his customers in 1789 was General James Wilkinson, who presumably used this whiskey as a part of his flatboat cargo on New Orleans-bound trips.[25]

At various times the relation of a church member with whiskey production was brought before the governing body of his church for official opinions. A representative question and decision were recorded in 1795: "Querry, is it Consistant with True religion and the Gospel of Christ for a member of a Church to Carry on a Distillery of Spirits. Answer'd Not Inconsistant."[26] A somewhat

[23] George W. Ranck, *History of Lexington, Kentucky* (Cincinnati, 1872), 301.

[24] Contemporary records from nearby states and frontier areas (Tennessee and North Carolina, for example) show this to be representative of the norm and not just a laxity peculiar to pleasure-loving Kentuckians. See Walter B. Posey, "The Frontier Baptist Ministry," *East Tennessee Historical Society Publications* 14 (1942): 3; Joseph R. Nixon, *The German Settlers in Lincoln County and Western North Carolina*, James Sprunt Historical Publications of the North Carolina Historical Society, 11, no. 2 (Chapel Hill, 1912): 42–43.

[25] Statement of General James Wilkinson's account with Lewis Craig, April 28, 1789, Innes Papers, fol. 23, part 1, 5111.

[26] Bryan's Station Church Minute Book, 1786–1895, 79. This spelling varies, Bryan, Bryan's, and Bryant's all being acceptable.

similar official opinion from another church in 1797 is quoted by Ward Russell: "Quere from Licking whether the Church is justifiable in shutting the door against a member of a Sister Church (that offers his membership) for the cause of retailing of Liquors agreeable to Law; answered No."[27]

Inasmuch as a considerable number of church members were engaged in the manufacture and merchandising of liquor, it is hardly surprising that the ecclesiastical attitude was tolerant. In 1798 various subscribers agreed "to give unto John Shackelford the different subscriptions against our names in the property mentioned . . . as a compensation for his services in the Minister in bounds for South Elkhorn Congregation." Three of the parties to this compact were committed to furnish a total of thirty-six gallons of whiskey.[28]

Occasionally, however, church members, both men and women, were formally charged with having been intoxicated or with the greater sin of outright drunkenness. Depending on the seriousness of the accusation or—apparently of more importance—the attitude of the accused, punishment ranged from a caution delivered by the moderator to exclusion from Communion or outright expulsion from the church. One errant brother at Bryan's Station "informed the Church that sometime past he was in Lexington great Excitement prevailing on the subject of Colora he having sempsoms [symptoms] drank some brandy found he had taken too much the Church voted Satisfaction on acknowledgment."[29] However, one repentant member from Clear Creek requested exclusion from his church because "he had gotten drunk, when he went to Lexington."[30]

Frontier "revival meetings" seem to have offered a particularly

---

[27] Ward Russell, *Church Life in the Blue Grass, 1783–1933* (Lexington, 1933), 42. See also J. H. Spencer, *A History of Kentucky Baptists, from 1769 to 1885* (Cincinnati, 1886), 2:15.

[28] Russell, *Church Life in the Blue Grass*, 42–43.

[29] Bryan's Station Church Minute Book, 1786–1895, 290.

[30] John Taylor, *A History of Ten Baptist Churches* (Frankfort, 1823), 57.

favorable market for the sale of liquor. The diary of the Reverend John Lyle, a Presbyterian minister, records disapprovingly two such instances. In one, "a Baptist member brought a wagon load of whiskey and sold it out. Many got groggy. One old Carr a Rankinite sold at his own house &c."[31] The other occurred at Springfield; "an old Baptist woman sold whiskey there and produced confusion as she had done at Paris."[32]

As in the older settlements, whiskey often figured in the expenses incurred for funerals. A Lincoln County funeral in 1783 produced the following charges against the estate of the deceased:

To plank for Coffin of Walnutt	5/6
For making of the Coffin	9/
For the nails for sd Coffin	2/6
For Two Gallons & one Quart of Whiskey @ 2 doll per	1/7[33]

The death of an individual, particularly if intestate, quite often led to an appraisal and sale of the effects. Here, as in the case of other crowd-generating social events such as elections and funerals, strong drink was one of the essential accessories. The sale of an estate in Mercer County in 1791 required approximately seven gallons of whiskey to fulfill this customary social obligation.[34] Many of the early Kentucky estates, while quite ordinary in all other respects, contained, upon inventory, considerable quantities of whiskey and brandy. On occasion, this constituted the most valuable item of the inventory. For example, a Mason County estate of 1798 was found to contain 169 gallons of these two distillates, valued at more than thirty-five pounds.[35]

[31] Quoted in Robert Stuart Sanders, *History of Walnut Hill Presbyterian Church* (Frankfort, 1956), 12.

[32] Quoted in Robert Stuart Sanders, *An Historical Sketch of Springfield Presbyterian Church* (Frankfort, 1954), 28.

[33] Lincoln County Will Book A, 56. The whiskey charge should undoubtedly be 1/7/0.

[34] Mercer County Will Book 1, 65; see also p. 172; Woodford County Will Book A, 103.

[35] Mason County Will Book A, 380–86. See also Mercer County Will

A reliance on spirits as a household commodity was another custom which had crossed the mountains with the early settlers. In reminiscing about his father, General Green Clay, Cassius Clay described what must have been a very stimulating pioneer custom: "But, in the morning, having a bottle of native 'Bourbon,' filled with camomile-flowers, which, being bitter, were used very generally as a tonic before breakfast, he would take out the bottle, fill his mouth with the hateful liquid, and, having swallowed it, make a rueful face at the boys; but he would drink no more that day."[36] The use of such an eye-opener seems to have been prevalent, not only in early Kentucky but in the South in general, where "a morning draught of either [peach or apple brandy] was considered as essential to good health as a breakfast."[37]

Somewhat reminiscent of medical practices in the two preceding centuries, those of the early nineteenth were also distinguished by a variety of remedies which featured distilled spirits. Travelers observed and reported on the widespread use of whiskey as a panacea for the ailments of mankind. On one occasion, during an epidemic of measles, several of the afflicted were "all drinking whiskey to excite perspiration."[38] Whiskey was also a favorite antidote against the effects of a soaking in a rainstorm.[39]

Alcoholic spirits represented the common and vital ingredient in favorite medicinal preparations used by Kentuckians—both internally and externally. Two recipes illustrate the customary dependence on spirits:

Book 1, 71; Lincoln County Will Book A, 77; Mason County Will Book A, 23; Madison County Will Book D, 493–97.

[36] Cassius Marcellus Clay, *The Life of Cassius Marcellus Clay: Memoirs, Writings and Speeches* (Cincinnati, 1886), 24. This was written long after the word "bourbon" had achieved common usage, and may be apocryphal.

[37] Edward R. Emerson, *Beverages, Past and Present* (New York, 1908), 2:462.

[38] Reuben Gold Thwaites, *Early Western Travels, 1748–1846* (Cleveland, 1904–1907), 3:151–52.

[39] Ibid., 4:207.

Receit for the Dropsy first . . . take 1 Pint Black Musterd seed two large Cullumba Beets 1 Large root of horsReddish 19 Eggshells Brown and powdr. 1 half Gill of peach Cenals put the hole of them into 1 half Gal. of Whiskey Drink as much as you can bare Day & night If this fails Repeat the same.[40]

Recipte for the Eyaws
Take 1 pint of hogs Lard
       1 handfull of Earth worms
       1 handfull of Tobacco
       4 pods of Red pepper
       1 Spunfill of Black pepper
       1 Race of Ginger
Stew them well together, & when Applyed mix Sum Sperits of Brandy with it.[41]

In 1820 the Danville press recommended a "recipe for indigestion, Colera Morbus, the Summer Complaint in children, or any complaint in the Stomach or Bowels." This all-round elixir was approved "for grown persons and children alike" and contained one-quarter pound of crude rhubarb, one-half ounce of caraway seed, and one-half ounce of orange peel "infused" in one quart of brandy.[42] During an outbreak of cholera in 1833, the Lexington press recommended a stimulating treatment: "If the patient is cramped, rub with hot Brandy and Cayenne Pepper. Keep the patient warm."[43]

The well-founded faith in the enlivening qualities of whiskey was justified in the case of a slaveowner moving to Kentucky with his human chattel: "When the slaves appeared about ready to quit, the Colonel came forward with his 'good friend whiskey' and gave them a portion each waking hour. Thus stimulated, they

[40] John B. Clark Papers, Kentucky Historical Society, Frankfort, fol. 173-A.
[41] Ibid.
[42] *Danville Olive Branch*, August 11, 1820. Hereafter cited as *Olive Branch*.
[43] *Lexington Observer and Kentucky Reporter*, June 1, 1833. Hereafter cited as *Observer and Kentucky Reporter*.

completed the journey without trouble."[44] Whiskey also sustained
the weary laborer, protecting him from occupational illnesses.
Ebenezer Hiram Stedman, describing his job at a paper mill in
Georgetown, Kentucky, (c. 1820) and its long working hours,
commented, "Then, i had to go to town for a Judg of whiskey, for
the men to drink next Day. Manny a night in Rain, Snow, & dark-
ness Have i packed that old Jug & in all My trips I never broke
one. . . . Paper Makers thought they Could not work without
whiskey. They had to have their hands & arms in the watter &
without whiskey they Said they woold take Cold. You will not Be
Surprised that i thought so too & i could drink To keep out Cold,
as Much as they Could.[45]

Whiskey was as useful as money, for which it frequently
served as substitute in frontier commerce. No other item, with the
possible exception of ginseng, represented such concentrated
value. Albert Gallatin, although referring to his neighbors in
western Pennsylvania at the time, could have included the Kentuckians in his petition to Congress (1792) against the excise:
"We are . . . distillers through necessity, . . . that we may
comprehend the greatest value in the smallest size and weight."[46]
Gallatin then referred to the distance from markets, the isolation
from the eastern coast on account of the mountains, the lack of
means to bring farm produce to profitable sale, and the scarcity
of cash which fostered the barter system—observations which
applied, to an even greater degree, to the Kentucky situation.[47] In
varying degrees, all of these shortcomings were to persist in the
economic life of Kentucky for many years to come. The experience
of Thomas Lincoln, Abraham's father, illustrates the situation in

[44] Lowell H. Harrison, "A Virginian Moves to Kentucky, 1793," *William
and Mary Quarterly* 3d ser., 15 (April 1958):208.

[45] Frances L. S. Dugan and Jacqueline P. Bull, eds., *Bluegrass Craftsman: Being the Reminiscences of Ebenezer Hiram Stedman, Papermaker,
1808–1885* (Lexington, 1959), 39–40.

[46] Henry Adams, *The Writings of Albert Gallatin* (Philadelphia,
1879), 1:3.

[47] Ibid., 3–4.

the fall of 1816. When he moved the family possessions from Kentucky to Indiana there were ten barrels of whiskey aboard his flatboat. He had "traded his farm for whisky, which was a kind of money in that day, and $20.00 cash."[48]

Through the first several decades of settlement, whiskey continued to be one of the principal media of exchange in Kentucky. The formation of a federal government seemingly provided little monetary relief; specie continued to remain scarce in frontier areas.[49] When Daniel Broadhead opened the first store in Louisville in the spring of 1783 he "took in pay for what he sold the produce of the country, such as peltry, tobacco, corn, whisky, linen and linsey, and got but little or no money."[50] Contemporary newspapers confirm the use of whiskey as an indispensable medium of exchange. An early issue of the Lexington *Gazette* announced that a new meeting house was to be erected in Danville; the notice informed prospective builders that "payment for building the said house, will be in stock and country produce, such as Cattle, Whiskey, wheat and rye."[51]

Daniel Drake's account of pre-1800 life in Mason County relates:

Through the period of which I write, Father aimed at raising horses for sale; and one of them proved to be very fine. Not satisfied with any price offered him at home, Father resolved to try a *foreign* market, & it was no other than the *adjoining* county of Bourbon. There he sold him to Mr.—afterwards Col. Garrard, a son of old Governor Garrard. In part pay, he took a hundred gallons of whisky. When it arrived we felt quite rich. A barrel

[48] Carl Sandburg, *Abraham Lincoln: the Prairie Years* (New York, 1926), 1:30; William Townsend, *Lincoln and Liquor* (New York, 1934), 12.

[49] Lewis Cecil Gray, *History of Agriculture in the Southern United States to 1860* (New York, 1941), 2:868.

[50] J. Stoddard Johnston, ed., *Memorial History of Louisville from Its First Settlement to the Year 1896* (Chicago, 1896), 1:51; see also Mann Butler, *A History of the Commonwealth of Kentucky* (Louisville, 1834), 142–43.

[51] *Gazette*, June 7, 1788.

was immediately tapped, and the "tin quart" scoured bright as possible, and put in requisition. Our customers were of course the neighbors, most of whom regarded it a duty to their families and visitors, not less than themselves, to keep the whiskey bottle well replenished. For a friend to call and find it empty was a real mortification to one party, and quite a disappointment to the other who was apt to revenge himself by speaking of the matter to some other neighbor as an instance of meanness, or (more accurately) of stinginess.[52]

Such was life in old Kentucky.

Well into the nineteenth century, whiskey figured prominently as an acceptable medium of exchange for both services and merchandise. All of the general stores solicited payment for dry goods and groceries in the produce of the country—whiskey in particular—in lieu of cash.[53] The specialty establishments did this also, and to a greater degree. Many notices offered for sale such diverse articles as saddles, Windsor chairs, ladies' hats, boots and shoes; in payment, whiskey was welcome.[54] In the Lexington *Gazette* Robert Sanders, himself a distiller, offered a reward of twenty pounds or 100 gallons of whiskey for the return of a runaway Negro slave.[55]

There seemed to be a natural affinity between whiskey and the stud fees of noted stallions and jacks. At any rate, among innumerable notices of sires standing at stud, whiskey was the commodity most generally specified as acceptable for payment. In 1792, for example, the stud fee for "the celebrated swift horse, Ferguson's Gray" was advertised as nine shillings payable in

[52] Daniel Drake, *Pioneer Life in Kentucky, 1785–1800*, ed. Emmet Field Horine (New York, 1948), 84. A public sale of Col. Garrard's estate involved "Between 80 and 100 barrels Whiskey," some "old Whiskey, Brandy, Wines," one set stills and tubs, and one set of cooper's tools. *Western Citizen*, September 14, 1838.

[53] See, for example, *Gazette*, March 15, 1790; *Patriot*, August 17, 1816; *Olive Branch*, June 23, 1820; *Frankfort Commentator*, June 14, 1828; hereafter cited as *Commentator*.

[54] *Gazette*, March 16, 1793; October 20, 1800; *Telegraph*, January 30, 1812; *Olive Branch*, November 18, 1820; *Western Herald*, May 10, 1826.

[55] *Gazette*, June 13, 1789.

merchantable whiskey (among other items of country produce).[56] Almost two decades later whiskey was acceptable for the services of "the celebrated Spanish Jack, Gayoso."[57] A comparison of these two notices with six others of a similar nature indicated that whiskey was the only desired article of country produce common to all.[58]

It is clear that the early Kentuckians, putting first things first, were keenly concerned with the eugenic breeding of horses. There was also concern, particularly in commercial circles, as to the welfare of the whiskey business. This was a time of struggle for survival in the economy of the new country, and postwar economic strains were nowhere felt more seriously than in the frontier settlements. Even while the First Congress of the United States was in session, the citizens of Danville were drawing up resolutions voicing the feelings of an "association of the inhabitants of this District against the use of foreign luxuries, &c."[59] Two of the resolutions, in particular, reflect their concern for the future of distilling in Kentucky:

. . . resolved to discard the unmanly fondness for the tinsel of European luxury and foppery . . . and after first day of February next, except in case of sickness, use any wine, rum, brandy, or other spiritous liquors which shall not be made within the District of Kentucky.

Resolved, That the present circumstances of the District are also adapted to the brewing of malt liquors, and to the distilling of spirits from grain and other subjects in such quantities as with proper attention and encouragement would be sufficient for general consumption.[60]

[56] Ibid., March 17, 1792.
[57] *Russellville Farmer's Friend*, May 25, 1810. Hereafter cited as *Farmer's Friend*.
[58] *Gazette*, October 20, 1800; February 28, March 6, 1804; March 5, 1805; March 29, 1806; *Correspondent*, March 20, 1815.
[59] *Gazette*, August 29, 1789.
[60] Ibid. The same type of action had been taken in western Pennsylvania in 1787; see R. E. Banta, *The Ohio* in *Rivers of America*, ed. Hervey Allen and Carl Carmer (New York, 1949), 191.

Competition from abroad was, however, far less of a problem to Kentuckians than was foreign control of the port of New Orleans. This control, first by Spain and then by France, threatened at any time to close the Mississippi River as an outlet for domestic production. Traffic on the Mississippi had begun at a relatively early date. A future Kentuckian, Captain Jacob Yoder, is credited with taking the first flatboat of produce from Redstone Fort to New Orleans in the spring of 1782, a pioneering venture which soon established the Mississippi as an indispensable outlet for Kentucky commodities.[61] Insofar as the distillers were concerned, there was good and sufficient reason for river transportation —the entire country to the east of the Kentucky District was adequately supplied with spirits of its own local manufacture.

Thus, the Kentucky settlers were to experience over three decades of uncertainty and, at times, outright frustration concerning the right to unrestricted navigation on the Mississippi. Awareness of this problem prompted the Lincoln County court to issue an unusual pronouncement in 1783:

Andrew M'Fagen a Gentleman of Good Charetor having an intention to travail Southwardly down the Messissippi on Mercantile business we desire that all persons may let him pass and repass about his lawful business and pay a due respect to him which is Justly due to his Charector, and also that his Assistants may be unmolested while in his service, they behaving themselves honestly and as good Citizens.[62]

This was undoubtedly the first passport ever issued by a Kentucky county—possibly the only one. Its effectiveness is not known, but there is no mistaking the underlying intent; the role of the "Mississippi" in early Kentucky commerce is made equally clear.

In the spring of 1787 General James Wilkinson made the first of several commercially important trips from the vicinity of Frank-

---

[61] John Mason Brown, *The Political Beginnings of Kentucky*, Filson Club Publications, no. 6 (Louisville, 1889), 87. See also Collins, *History of Kentucky*, 2:723.
[62] Lincoln County Order Book 1, 103–04.

fort to New Orleans. His boats were loaded with Kentucky produce, and in spite of impediments by the Spanish authorities, the venture was successful enough to encourage other traders.[63] One of General Wilkinson's partners, the versatile Peyton Short in Fayette County, owned a distillery and very probably furnished part of Wilkinson's cargoes.[64]

In spite of the lack of a definitive treaty with Spain, the river trade continued to grow. In 1792, John Moylan of Lexington advertised for several "hands" to work his boats down to New Orleans at the end of the year.[65] Like Moylan, many store owners of the time accumulated, through barter, quantities of country produce (including whiskey) and subsequently loaded boats for the river trade.[66] The Lexington firm of Irwin and Bryson advertised in 1793 that they wanted "a number of able bodied men to navigate their boats to New Orleans, good wages will be given, wholesome provisions provided and a sufficient quantity of whiskey allowed."[67] Advertisements of this type were common, and after Pinckney's Treaty with Spain (October 1795), their frequency increased. Upon news of the treaty, the Lexington *Gazette* recorded that "the general joy of all ranks and descriptions of citizens, was never so conspicuous as on the above occasion; of which, the firing of artillery, tolling of bells, bonfires, &c. &c. were evident testimony."[68]

In the downriver shipments of Kentucky whiskey, a substantial portion of the cargo normally disappeared en route, either by off-

[63] Thomas Robson Hay and M. R. Werner, *The Admirable Trumpeter: A Biography of General James Wilkinson* (Garden City, N.Y., 1941), 83; Royal Ornan Shreve, *The Finished Scoundrel* [General James Wilkinson] (Indianapolis, 1933), 64–65. For Pinckney Treaty, see Hunter Miller, ed., *Treaties and Other International Acts of the United States of America* (Washington, D.C., 1931–1948), 2:318–38.

[64] Hay and Werner, *Admirable Trumpeter*, 100, 108; Shreve, *Finished Scoundrel*, 82. For Short's distilling interest, see *Gazette*, January 28, 1791; May 26, 1792.

[65] *Gazette*, December 1, 1792.

[66] See ibid., November 24, 1792; January 5, 1793.

[67] Ibid., February 2, 1793.

[68] Ibid., March 26, 1796.

shore trading or internal consumption. In 1806 a Kentuckian, John Stuart, set out for New Orleans from Cleveland landing in Fayette County "with 315 barrels of flour whiskey & tobo [tobacco] rang'd in triple & quadruple tiers on each side of our boat."[69] About seventy miles below Louisville, Stuart recorded that "2 Indians came out to us. I bought a couple of fine Venison hams of them for ½ Gallon of Whiskey. they could scarcely speak a word of English."[70] He also recounted the excessive drinking on the part of the boatmen (including the owner) which took place during the voyage; the entire trip consumed slightly over three months.[71]

The disposal of Kentucky whiskey continued to follow a similar pattern for several decades. In 1808 the Lexington merchants James and Henry Wier included a considerable quantity of whiskey in a flatboat loaded with produce for the New Orleans market. Their instructions to the boat captain regarding the liquor were "to make sale of the property as he descends the River. should he not effect a sale of the Whole he is to deliver the balance."[72] This was typical of an established practice; the three-month voyage was actually a succession of stopovers at remote towns and landings between Kentucky and New Orleans.

For almost three and a half decades the firm of Fountain and Roderick Perry in Campbell County was involved in the Mississippi River commerce, of which whiskey was a sizeable component. In 1828, as captain of the appropriately named flatboat *Bachelors Joy*, Fountain Perry left Riddles Ferry with a cargo of tobacco, pork, lard, gunpowder, and twenty-five barrels of his own whiskey. His load also included a separate shipment of whiskey, together with instructions from the owner relative to its disposal: "Mr. Perry will sell the Whiskey if possible at prices over Thirty three cents should any remain on hand when the Boat

[69] John G. Stuart, "A Journal Remarks or Observations in a Voyage Down the Kentucky, Ohio, Mississippi Rivers, &c.," *Register of the Kentucky Historical Society* 50 (January 1952): 6.

[70] Ibid., 16.

[71] Ibid., 9–12.

[72] Draper Manuscripts, 21 CC 20.

arrives at Natches he will store it with Messrs Harris & March Commission Merchants."[73] Mr. Perry's consignment was duly receipted: "Rec! Cincin. Novr. 21, 1828. In Good order and well conditioned from Geo. Graham Jr. on board of my Flat Boat now at Cincinnati Thirty Barrels containing Ten hundred twelve Gallons Proof Whiskey which I am to sell to the best advantage and make return of Sales allowing a reasonable time for a coasting Voyage between Cincinnati and Natches or New Orleans deducting one Dollar and Fifty cents freight and Commission on each Barrel."[74] It would appear that Mr. Graham was unduly optimistic, or perhaps overly trustful. A receipt dated December 30, 1828, indicates that the entire thirty barrels of Graham whiskey were delivered at Natchez, but among the papers of Fountain Perry is an account of the trip showing many entries for sales of his own whiskey along the way.[75]

The growing economic importance of distilled spirits to Kentuckians may be judged by the volume of whiskey traffic on the Ohio and Mississippi rivers. In 1800, tobacco and whiskey replaced flour as the principal export crops from the interior of Kentucky.[76] During a three and one-half month period at the beginning of 1801 almost 50,000 gallons of distilled spirits, with an aggregate value of almost $29,000, were entered for exportation at the Louisville Custom House.[77] Somewhat over a decade later, a sizeable increase in this traffic had been noted. Zadok Cramer reported "receipts from the upper country" of 3,671 barrels of whiskey (considerably in excess of 110,000 gallons) at New Orleans for the first five months of 1812.[78]

Although Custom House figures are useful indications of whiskey traffic at the time, they are by no means comprehensive.

[73] Fountain and Roderick Perry Papers, University of Kentucky Library, Lexington, fol. 61 M 145.
[74] Ibid.
[75] Ibid.
[76] Staples, *History of Pioneer Lexington*, 158.
[77] *Gazette*, May 18, 1801.
[78] Zadok Cramer, *Cramer's Pittsburgh Almanac*, no. 12 (Pittsburgh, 1813), 56.

There were many accesses to the Mississippi, other than through Louisville and the Ohio River, from the interior of Kentucky. Several large streams, suitable for flatboat navigation, enter the Ohio and Mississippi well below the Falls—for example, the Cumberland, Tennessee, Salt, and Green rivers. William Flinn Rogers reported that before the end of the eighteenth century the production of the East Tennessee distillers was being loaded on twenty-ton boats in the Knoxville area (Tennessee River), destined for the Mississippi trade.[79]

As an indicator of the export of Kentucky whiskey, compilations of figures from places downstream are equally misleading, for these usually included the receipts from areas other than Kentucky. Many states which produced significant quantities of distilled spirits in the period had adequate access to Mississippi River commerce. For example, in 1810, when Kentucky produced 2,220,773 gallons of distilled spirits, Pennsylvania produced 6,552,284 gallons; Virginia, 2,367,589 gallons; North Carolina, 1,386,691 gallons; Ohio, 1,212,266 gallons; and Tennessee, 801,245 gallons.[80] Kentucky, with 2,000 stills, was exceeded in that category by North Carolina, Virginia, and Pennsylvania—in that order; the total value of spirits distilled in Kentucky, $740,242, was also exceeded by the same three states and closely followed by Ohio and Tennessee.[81]

[79] William Flinn Rogers, "Life in East Tennessee Near End of Eighteenth Century," *East Tennessee Historical Society Publications* 1(1929): 38.

[80] Tench Coxe, *A Statement of the Arts and Manufactures of the United States of America, for the Year 1810* (Philadelphia, 1814), 22.

[81] Ibid.

5

A Hateful Tax

A s we have seen, when whiskey came to Kentucky it already had a long history of involvement in American life. Government after government, surveying this frisky product, had sensed in its traffic a need of regulation. It was soon to show its capacity to justify and sustain a busy bureaucracy. Increasingly, the flowing bowl had been garnished with imposts, excises, licenses, and ordinances. Still, as any officeholder would have acknowledged, expensive wars had to be financed, statehouses and governors' mansions had to be erected, roads and canals and schoolhouses were urgently needed—in short, nation-building was an expensive business. Liquor, ever useful, helped to pay the bill.

The attempted regulation of strong drink in America was almost as old as the first colony; an act to restrict drunkenness had been passed by the Virginia Assembly in 1619. Licenses were regularly issued in Virginia and the other colonies for operating the ordinary or tavern (restraint of tippling houses), for distilling, for selling liquor by "ye small measure," and for selling spirits to the Indians. Certainly a common characteristic of the original thirteen colonies was the periodic enactment of measures similar (or identical) to the foregoing. The achievement of independence produced no significant changes in this respect; the several states continued to enact such controls. Even the short-lived State of Franklin assigned prices to various commodities, including "good, distilled Rye Whiskey."[1]

During the first decade and a half of Kentucky settlement the Virginia legislature entrusted liquor control to the county courts, through local enactments. Under frontier conditions this control could, of course, be rendered ineffective by the sympathetic attitude of enforcement officials or by the insufficient number of functioning courts. Nevertheless, the initial court enactments of all Virginia-created counties included some form of liquor control.

Following Kentucky's elevation to statehood (June 1, 1792), one of the earlier acts passed by its General Assembly was "An Act to Regulate Taverns and Restrain Tippling Houses."[2] This statute provided, among other things, for the periodic establishment of rates by justices of the county courts, the licensing and bonding of tavern keepers, and penalties for overcharging. However, there was no attempt by the state to provide for any restrictions on distilled spirits other than social control of usage: there were no direct taxes on the product.

When the first excise tax was imposed, it encountered a vigorous, though belated, opposition in Kentucky. Distillers were completely unaccustomed to a centralized American government armed with coercive powers. There had been no effective attempt at excise taxation on the part of the government under the Articles of Confederation, nor would uniform enforcement of such measures have been possible.

The Excise Act was passed on March 3, 1791, to become operational on the following July 1.[3] The new law provided for progressive duties, ranging from nine to twenty-five cents per gallon and scaled to six classes of proof, on all spirits "distilled within the United States, from any article of the growth and

---

[1] Oliver Taylor, *Historic Sullivan: A History of Sullivan County, Tennessee* (Bristol, 1909), 112. This experiment in state making lasted for approximately four years, ending when North Carolina reestablished jurisdiction in 1789.

[2] William Littell, comp., *The Statute Law of Kentucky* (Frankfort, 1809–1819), 1:194–97. For subsequent enactments of a similar nature, see William Littell and Jacob Swigert, comps., *A Digest of the Statute Law of Kentucky* (Frankfort, 1822), 2:1186–88.

[3] U.S., *Statutes at Large*, 1:199–214.

produce of the United States, in any city, town or village." For country stills, the law specified a yearly duty of sixty cents per gallon of still capacity (including the head), with an option to the owner of paying nine cents per gallon on actual production instead of potential output. Equally onerous were other provisions requiring relatively complicated bookkeeping, identification marks on buildings and equipment used for distilling, and full cooperation with the federal inspectors, including "entry" (registry) of such buildings and stills prior to their usage.[4]

The triumphant march of bureaucracy began without delay, as President Washington divided the United States into fourteen districts of administration. The State of Virginia was designated as the Eleventh District and subdivided into seven surveys of inspection, of which Kentucky was Survey Number Seven. Thomas Marshall of Woodford County, father of a future Chief Justice, was designated inspector of the Kentucky survey at a salary of $450 per year and a commission of 1 percent on collections. Compensation to the prospective "Collectors of the Revenue" was established at 4 percent commission on collections of duties on spirits distilled from domestic materials.[5]

Marshall, himself a distiller, lost no time in spreading the glad news. The following appeared in the June 18 Lexington *Gazette:*

Notice is given to the distillers of spirits in the district of Kentucky that the act of Congreess [*sic*] laying a duty on Stills or distilled spirits will take place on the first day of July next, and as there are several penalties and forfeitures in the said act, which may be incurred by them, for want of a knowledge of the requisites directed by the same previous to the payment of said duties. I think it proper and necessary to inform them, that I have the act and shall be ready to shew it at my house to any person desirous of being acquainted with its contents.[6]

⁴ Ibid.; U.S., *American State Papers, Finance*, 1:110–11.
⁵ John C. Fitzpatrick, *The Writings of George Washington from the Original Manuscript Sources, 1745–1799* (Washington, D.C., 1931–1941), 31:233–40.
⁶ *Gazette*, June 18, 1791. For evidence of Thomas Marshall's distilling interests, see *Gazette*, October 3, 1799.

Judging from the evidence, it is doubtful if many of the Kentucky distillers were overly concerned with the implications of this intelligence—at the onset. There certainly was no significant increase in newspaper publicity relative to the sale of distilling equipment. Peyton Short, the owner of distilleries in both Woodford and Fayette counties, advertised his properties for lease and sale respectively, but this action was undoubtedly prompted by his appointment as revenue collector for Louisville, rather than by concern over the excise.[7] Another Woodford County citizen, John Grant, offered a tract of land including a distillery, but did not indicate tax apprehension as the reason.[8]

In view of the obvious threat to the welfare and profits of the Kentucky distillers, their initial apathy is hard to understand. Theirs, however, was an age of happy ignorance of the galloping ways of federal coercion, and this unawareness was compounded by the typical disrespect of the backwoodsman toward all forms of authority. Marshall was aware of this attitude, and in March 1792, announcing the appointment of tax collectors for the (then) nine existing counties of the state, he spoke very firmly:

Some of the distillers I am informed, pretend to say they are taught to believe that the excise is not to be collected in this district. From whence they derive their information I cannot conceive; but do hereby inform them that the collectors will shortly be with them in order to collect it, and that those who are not provided with money, or shew a disposition to oppose the execution of the law will be proceeded against as that law directs.[9]

There had obviously been much loose talk and threats to disregard the excise in Kentucky. It is doubtful that readers of the Lexington *Gazette* were greatly soothed, either, by "Observations on the excise law, being an extract of a letter from a gentleman in Virginia to his friend in Kentucky." This literary effort questioned

[7] Ibid., June 25, 1791; January 28, 1792. For Peyton Short's appointment, see ibid., October 10, 1789.
[8] Ibid., August 19, 1791.
[9] Ibid., March 17, 1792.

the conduct of the citizenry and lectured them on the necessity of taxes for the support of government, including some gratuitous information on the benefits which the state received from the central government.[10]

Shortly after Marshall's warning in March, the distillers in Fayette County made an effort toward concerted protest:

NOTICE That the distillers in the district of Kentucky are earnestly requested to attend at the Court House in Lexington, on the Monday before the Next Fayette Couurt [sic]—this meeting is thought highly necessary, as some general and unanimous measures may be adopted amongst them respecting the Excise law, and the operation thereof.[11]

It is doubtful, however, that this meeting and others of a similar nature were completely representative of the Kentucky distillers. Distance alone would have militated against attendance other than from Fayette County and its immediate environs.

Distillers throughout the nation expressed such dissatisfaction with the original excise law that Congress was prompted to enact a modification, partially answering some of the most pointed objections. Kentucky's contribution to the general unrest was of sufficient intensity that it received official recognition from the commissioner of revenue. Writing to the secretary of the treasury in May of 1792, Tench Coxe referred to Marshall's letters which "shew an uneasiness about the Revenue law to exist in part of Kentucky. The New Act will diminish their opposition, because it is so much more favorable to them than the former, & because it proves that there is no Idea of a Repeal."[12] The new regulations provided a graduated reduction in duties on the six classes of proof, ranging from two to seven cents per gallon. For country stills and any others whose total capacity was less than four hundred gallons, there were provided three optional forms of pay-

[10] Ibid.

[11] Ibid., April 28, 1792

[12] Harold C. Syrett, ed., *The Papers of Alexander Hamilton* (in progress; New York, 1961–   ), 11:407.

ment: an annual tax of fifty-four cents per gallon on total capacity, or seven cents per gallon for every gallon of spirits distilled, or ten cents per gallon of capacity for each month the still was in use.[13] It is obvious that this compromise was designed to pacify the distillers of the western country; few of them, if any, possessed stills in excess of this size. Subscribers to the Lexington *Gazette* were informed of this development in July of 1792.[14]

Thomas Marshall's administrative headaches were not all related to the reluctant distillers in his district; on many occasions he was compelled to remind the revenue collectors of their sworn obligations:

. . . unless they proceed immediately to the execution of the duties of their several offices, and collect indiscriminately from all persons chargeable with the excise, the sums which they owe, as well for the last as the present year, that their bonds shall be forthwith put in suit to reimburse the United States for the loss their negligence may occasion. Should they meet with any opposition in the collection for either year, they are directed to instruct the Attorney General for the United States to prosecute the delinquents for the penalties they may have rendered themselves liable to.[15]

In November of 1792, Marshall publicly listed the tax collectors for nine of the thirteen existing counties; in so doing he revealed one of the roots of his difficulties. No collectors were listed for the counties of Bourbon, Shelby, Logan, and Mason, all areas of considerable size; it is obvious where many of the delinquent distillers were located.[16] The growth of bureaucracy, while certainly prompt enough for most of the distillers, had not adequately covered the state. A similar notice at the beginning of 1793 failed to include collectors for these four counties; nor was

---

[13] U.S., *Statutes at Large*, 1:267–71.

[14] *Gazette*, July 14, 1792.

[15] Ibid., November 24, 1792. This notice appeared in several consecutive issues.

[16] Ibid.

there any mention of collectors for the new counties of Clark, Hardin, and Green—all created in December of 1792.[17]

The distillers of Survey Number Seven received another admonition from Marshall late in 1792, typical of the constant stream of warnings emanating from the tax authorities:

A great indulgence having been already given to the distillers within this Commonwealth, and the time being near at hand when they are to account with the collectors of the several divisions for the revenue in their hands; I have directed the collectors to pay the most strict attention to the duties of their office, as no possible indulgence can be given in future inconsistent with the interest of the United States.[18]

Through issue after issue of the Lexington *Gazette*, one can detect the ceaseless tides of battle in central Kentucky between the swooping revenue agents and the stubborn, evasive, and downright uncooperative distillers. Throughout the period of the first excise, the government threatened and exhorted. It announced a virtual ultimatum for immediate payment of arrearages; it hinted of leniency and forgiveness of past lapses; it threatened to visit retribution upon guilty citizens; it moaned continuingly of delinquencies of distillers and tax collectors alike. Collectively, these allusions add up to one thing—an eleven-year campaign of deliberate tax evasion by a sizeable number of Kentucky distillers. Nor was this misconduct confined to Fayette County, which, with its own newspaper, gave publicity to the problem; vast areas of the state had no newspaper at all and no tax collectors.

An unsigned notice in the *Gazette* for June of 1793 requested "that all the distillers or their respective agents in this state, attend at Lexington on Monday the 8th of July ensuing, to consult on measures to be taken relative to the payment of the excise on spirits distilled within the state."[19] The resulting meeting was

[17] Ibid., January 5, 1793.
[18] Ibid., November 24, 1792.
[19] Ibid., June 1, 1793.

attended by a total of eight persons, giving credence to Humphrey Marshall's accusation that "the influence of a few individuals" was responsible for the rebellious spirit manifested in Kentucky.[20] However, the opinions expressed at this assemblage represented the basic reasons for discontent among the western people in general and distillers in particular:

. . . that collecting taxes under the excise law in specie only, will be oppressive to the people of this country, in our present situation, as we cannot carry our produce to market through the channel of the Mississippi. . . . are of opinion it [excise] is unjust, because our navigation is stopt (by the Spaniards) which is our natural and constitutional right; while the other states in the union have their ports open, and can sell their produce for specie; and as allegiance and protection are reciprocal, the United States ought to see that we are equally protected in our trade before we are expected to pay equal taxes under the excise law in specie only. . . . If we were allowed to pay our taxes under the excise law in produce at a reasonable price, it would be more just, though not fully so; . . . our former petition or memorial to Congress concerning this business, was laid on the table and neglected; . . . we are as a barrier to part of the other states against the savages, sustaining such damages as we do by their murthering and plundering our people to a very great amount in every year.—Our trade being stopped—our country but very little improved, and of course we cannot have cyder and beer as substitutes for spirits distilled, as the people have in the old country.[21]

Some of these grievances were valid enough, but the memorial considerably overstates its case. Spanish restrictions were not as stringent as this lament would indicate; a mere ten months earlier, at least six local firms had sought hired help to work their boats to New Orleans. Furthermore, there is every reason to doubt that

[20] Humphrey Marshall, *History of Kentucky* (Frankfort, 1824), 2:124. In addition to being one of Kentucky's first historians, Humphrey Marshall was also a nephew of Thomas Marshall, the revenue supervisor. See Allen Johnson and Dumas Malone, eds., *Dictionary of American Biography* (New York, 1943), 12:309–10.

[21] *Gazette*, August 10, 1793.

cider and beer were unavailable to Kentuckians at the time. They had been growing fruit since 1775, and by 1795 most of the farms offered for sale had orchards of considerable size. Beer breweries had been in existence since well before 1790, both in Lexington and in other parts of the state.[22] The "brewing of malt liquors" had been one of the features for which "the present circumstances of the District are also adapted" in the resolutions of 1789.

The content of Marshall's communication to his agents in June of 1794 reveals the deplorable extent of arrearages in revenue affairs:

The several Collectors of Revenue on Spirits distilled in the State of Kentucky (7th survey for the district of Virginia) heretofore appointed, are hereby requested to attend the inspector of revenue for the said survey at his office, on some day between the 15th and 20th of July next, for the purpose of settling their respective accounts for the years 1791, 1792, 1793, and up to the first day of July 1794, and receive new commissions for the next twelve months, commencing on the said first day of July 1794, and ending on the last day of June 1795, and to do and perform all further requisites of the law.[23]

Further modifications of the Excise Act were passed in June 1794, allowing state and territorial courts to exercise concurrent jurisdiction in areas more than fifty miles distant from the federal courts. The new regulation also provided that additional districts and surveys could be opened "to facilitate and secure the collection of the revenue on distilled spirits, and stills, in such states as have been, or hereafter may be erected, and in the territories northwest, and south of the river Ohio."[24] A new administrative unit, the District of Ohio, was accordingly created, and an Office of In-

[22] See ibid., September 12, 1789; January 28, July 28, 1792; February 9, 1793.

[23] Ibid., June 28, 1794. Statement of revenue from stills and spirits distilled in the United States, for fiscal year 1794–1795 has no return from Marshall. U.S., *American State Papers, Finance*, 1:390.

[24] U.S., *Statutes at Large*, 1:378–81.

spection was opened in Cincinnati for the Number Two Survey.[25] Apparently this move closed one of the existing tax loopholes, for in the following month the revenue offices for this survey announced the sale at public auction of "two boats together with their cargoes, containing about sixteen hundred gallons of whiskey, &c."[26]

The Whiskey Rebellion in the four western counties of Pennsylvania was unquestionably the high point in national resistance to the excise laws, but it was by no means the only resort to force in preventing the execution of tax collections on distilled spirits.[27] As early as February 1794 the federal employees in Kentucky were experiencing treatment similar to that accorded their colleagues in western Pennsylvania. There were, for instance, the tribulations of William Hubble, collector of the revenue for the counties of Bourbon and Mason. On the seventh of February, Hubble was robbed of a considerable amount of personal property including "a pair of large square Saddle-bags, containing the following articles, viz. . . . a number of papers concerning the revenue of the United States; also a number of accounts rendered to the United States, upon stills and distilled spirits, within the counties of Bourbon and Mason: and upwards of one hundred and fifty dollars in money."[28]

Humphrey Marshall offered his own interpretation of the resistance in Kentucky:

While these proceedings [in Pennsylvania] were carefully and anxiously watched by the malcontents in this state, they were imitated, with the more caution, as they were seen at a distance,

[25] The District of Ohio was formed August 20, 1794. U.S., *American State Papers, Finance*, 1:390; see also *Centinel*, March 28, 1795. Thomas Marshall continued as supervisor of the new district.

[26] *Centinel*, April 4, 1795.

[27] The standard work on the Whiskey Rebellion is Leland D. Baldwin, *Whiskey Rebels: The Story of a Frontier Uprising* (Pittsburgh, 1939). For a more recent account, of revisionist nature, see Jacob E. Cooke, "The Whiskey Insurrection: A Re-evaluation," *Pennsylvania History* 30 (July 1963):316–46.

[28] *Gazette*, February 22, 1794.

and it was suggested of them, as being obvious, that government would be compelled to interfere—the result of which, at the time, although doubtful, could not be contemplated without apprehension. There was also the less occasion for a forcible opposition in Kentucky, as George Nicholas had undertaken, in the character of lawyer for distillers, to prevent judgments against them for infractions of the law; and Judge Innis [Harry Innes], who alone held the court, was contented that the law should not be executed.[29]

It was further recounted by Marshall that as the whiskey rebels "progressed in insubordination, so did Kentucky; but at an humble distance, in the rear. By the time, the Pennsylvanians had arrived at arming, against the government; some of the Kentucky distillers, ventured to black themselves, and assault an exciseman."[30] Temple Bodley's description of the resistance also suggests that the Kentuckians offered a more violent opposition than they are usually credited with: "[Thomas Marshall] was 'burned in effigy at Lexington'; 'collectors were assaulted; some received insulting and abusive language; others had their papers destroyed, their horses' ears cropped, manes and tails close shaves, their saddles cut to pieces; and such was the general abuse that very few were found hardy enough to undertake the office.' "[31]

The unsympathetic Humphrey Marshall described the outcome of the short-lived Pennsylvania rebellion:

For some time, it was propagated by the leaders, that the citizens, of the United States could never be brought to take up arms against their fellow citizens, for resisting the obnoxious laws of the general government. And great expectations were excited, and rested, for a while, upon this suggestion. The time now approached, when it was to be put to the test. . . . The march of these citizen soldiers, across the mountains, resolved the problem which had been projected by disaffection to the government, in

[29] Marshall, *History of Kentucky*, 2:124.
[30] Ibid., 156–57.
[31] Temple Bodley and Samuel M. Wilson, *History of Kentucky* (Chicago, 1928), 1:501. Kentucky opposition to the excise received official recognition at the time. See U.S., *American State Papers, Finance*, 1:279.

a manner, appalling to its destined object; and with the happiest effect on the democratic patriots of Kentucky.[32]

District court records testify to some of this violence and tend to vindicate Humphrey Marshall's charges of lenience on the part of Lawyer Nicholas and Judge Innes. Two Fayette County distillers were charged with "forceably obstructing on the 15th day of Feb'y, 1795 . . . William Sthreshly [sic] an Officer of Inspection in execution of his duty in marking and numbering [stills]." The grand jury presentments in these cases were made over twenty-two months later; one of the accused had died before his case came to trial. When the other case came up, it was discovered that they had the wrong man.[33] William Hubble, another officer of inspection, was "forcibly obstructed" in Harrison County by an obstreperous distiller in February of 1797. Over a year later the case was discontinued, with the defendant paying the costs; the case had been "continued to next court" on two interim occasions.[34] Another inspector, Thomas Streshly, was the plaintiff in a case of assault and battery in 1797; this case was later quashed for "informality."[35]

One curious development in Kentucky at the peak of the unrest was a practice inaugurated by the federal government; the revenue collectors became also, in effect, purchasing agents for the army. This scheme of collateral stewardships was a guileful one, as was revealed in the announcements of Collector Thomas Carneal early in 1795. His preliminary notification stated that he wanted "a quantity of WHISKEY, for the use of the army, for which CASH will be offered in payment."[36] Two weeks later Carneal elaborated:

Whiskey Wanted. I want to purchase a quantity of *legal distilled Whiskey*, for the use of the U.S. army North West of the Ohio.

---

[32] Marshall, *History of Kentucky*, 2:157.
[33] U.S., District Court Records, Kentucky District, 1789–1800, section 1, 142, 147, 162, 170, 212.
[34] Ibid., 147, 165, 168, 181.
[35] Ibid., 147, 162, 171.
[36] *Gazette*, January 3, 1795.

Whiskey will be received at 57 Cents per gallon, in payment of arrears of taxes on Spirits distilled in the State of Kentucky since the first of July 1791. And all the Distillers within this State who wish to close their accounts on the above terms, will apply at my Office in Lexington, between this and the 15th of February next, after which I shall not consider myself bound to take Whiskey in payment, and shall contract privately with individuals for the remaining quantity which may then be wanted.

N. B. The time and place of delivery, will be made convenient to the distillers.[37]

Such a blending of bureaucratic functions could be profitable to the officeholder, as suggested in Collector William Sthreshly's [*sic*] advertisement of 1796: "I want to purchase a quantity of Corn, Rye, and legal distilled WHISKEY; for which I will give a good price if delivered at my store in Lexington."[38] This Bluegrass bureaucrat was doubly armed with federal powers of confiscation and purchase, and was in an excellent position to regulate the prices of the distillers with whom he dealt. Judging from his notice of grains wanted, he himself was involved in the distilling business.[39]

In the brief period of three years (1794–1797) there occurred several events, both domestic and international, which combined to alleviate some of the more pressing of the western grievances. General Wayne's victory at Fallen Timbers in August 1794 and, twelve months later, the resulting Treaty of Greenville had the practical effect of settling once and for all the Kentuckians' Indian problem which had persisted for twenty years. In the Jay Treaty of 1794 the British had agreed to evacuate the northwest forts, and the Pinckney Treaty with Spain in 1795 assured the long-coveted freedom of access to the Mississippi trade. A salutary result of the Whiskey Rebellion, which also settled temporarily the question of federal supremacy, had been the importation of large quantities of specie into disaffected areas—particularly into

[37] Ibid., January 17, 1795. Italics added.
[38] Ibid., January 23, 1796.
[39] Ibid., June 20, 1795; January 23, 1796.

western Pennsylvania—through large-scale purchase of whiskey for military rations.[40] An additional modification in the excise in 1797 abolished the optional provision which had allowed the payment of seven cents per gallon for country stills of less than 400 gallons combined capacity. This was replaced with the option of obtaining a license for any one of seven periods scaled from two weeks to six months, at fees ranging from six cents to forty-two cents per gallon of capacity.[41]

However many the improvements in the western situation, the far-ranging supervision of the federal government continued to bedevil the Kentucky distillers; it finally aroused the ire of a worthy antagonist, none other than the former governor, Isaac Shelby. Shelby's letter of October 15, 1796, to the secretary of the treasury, Oliver Wolcott, is illustrative of several fairly common complaints on the part of Kentucky distillers and several inherent weaknesses in the excise system:

Sir
I have been informed, that in a letter addressed by you during the last session of congress to the chairman of a committee of the house of representatives, you stated, "that for want of a district attorney in Kentucky, no duties could be collected; that the governor himself refused to pay; and that the people sheltered themselves under his example." For the satisfaction of the public, I shall state a few facts concerning this business:—I rented out my distillery in August 1792, previous to which no application had been made to me by any excise officer to measure my stills or to take an entry of them: I continued to rent out my stills from that time until the latter end of the year 1793, and the tenants gave me their bonds to keep me idemnified from any demands that might be made on me for the excise during that period: I then took them again into my possession and commenced working of them in January, 1794. About the month of April following I was applied to by an excise officer (for the first time) for the duties of

---

[40] Leland D. Baldwin, "Orders Issued by General Henry Lee during the Campaign against the Whiskey Insurrectionists," *Western Pennsylvania Historical Magazine* 19 (June 1936):88, 98, 99, 106.
[41] U.S., *Statutes at Large*, 1:504–05.

that year. I informed him of the time I had taken my distillery into possession and that I did not conceive any duties could then be due from the time I had commenced working my distillery, which he appeared satisfied with.—He removed shortly afterward out of the country, and there was not to my knowledge any excise officer in it until about the month of January or February, 1795. I was then called upon to make an entry of my stills from June 1794, which I did immediately: after I had done this, the officer asked me if I would pay the arrearages. I told him I did not know whether the law required it of me; that I would take council on the subject, and that if I found that the law did require it of me, that I would pay them on the first application; otherwise I would not. He said he was not bound to call a second time to demand them: I told him if he did not choose to do so, he might execute his duty immediately and take my property. This he did not do but went away. I was shortly afterwards advised that the law would not compel me to pay the arrearages; but when the duties from June 1794 to June 1795 become [sic] due, I counted out and laid by itself the amount of what was due from me for that period, that the officer when he called again, might have occasion to stay as short a time as possible in my house. No application of any kind has since that time been made to me by any excise officer; and I found upon enquiry, that I could not procure a permit to remove whiskey which I had distilled between June 1794 and June 1795, owing to the want of an officer in the county. I have very lately been obliged to apply personally to the officer who is at this time acting in the county, to receive the taxes due from me for that period, and from June 1795 to June 1796.

From this statement of facts, the public will find that your assertion as far as it concerns me, is false; and I believe it to be equally groundless as far as it concerns the distillers in general within this state. I have no doubt but that it will be found, upon an impartial enquiry, that the distillers have paid considerable sums on account of the excise; and that it has been owing to the neglect or misconduct of the officers of government, that the duties have not been universally collected from June 1794.

It is a matter of indifference to me whether you fabricated your false statement yourself or received it from others, having made it, you are responsible for the truth of it: but, as the distance between us renders a personal application to you impracticable, I shall upon this and all future occasions, where you may use my name improperly, take the liberty of assuring you in this public manner, that I despise you most heartily.

Isaac Shelby[42]

Shortly before his resignation in 1797, the long-suffering supervisor of the revenue made yet another effort at obtaining cooperation from the reluctant distillers of Kentucky. In compliance with instructions received from Philadelphia, Marshall accordingly publicized the latest official position in the matter:

. . . the first demands ought to be made of those delinquents whose example in opposition to the law has been most influential. If they shall manifest a disposition to submit to the law, by complying with any formal injunctions before omitted, and shall agree to pay the duties which shall have accrued, for two years prior to the first day of July 1797, the Supervisor ought to settle with them on those terms, without coercing the penalties, or the former arrears. . . . If a disposition to a compromise shall not be perceived among the influential non-compliers with the law, suits ought to be commenced against this class of men generally; with respect to men of inferior consideration and influence, suits may be suspended until further instructions are received.[43]

Marshall's successor as supervisor for the Ohio District was Major James Morrison of Lexington, a former member of the Kentucky Assembly from Fayette County.[44] Along with the office, Morrison inherited its problems, and the stream of published pleas, threats, and admonishments continued.[45] As before, a great many distillers persisted in their noncooperative ways: they would not make entry of their stills, nor would they pay the required duties. In November 1797, the secretary of the treasury reported

[42] Stewart's Kentucky Herald, November 8, 1796; Gazette, November 12, 1796.

[43] Gazette, May 6, 1797. Thomas Marshall resigned as supervisor of the revenue on June 30, 1797, "because of age and infirmity." Johnson and Malone, Dictionary of American Biography, 12:328–29.

[44] Richard H. Collins, History of Kentucky (Covington, 1874), 2:170, 772. James Morrison also had distilling interests; see Gazette, April 19, 1803.

[45] Gazette, September 2, 1797; June 13, 1798; May 2, 1799.

for the fiscal year a gross revenue from stills and distilled spirits of $890,839, exclusive of amounts due "principally from Ohio and Pennsylvania." In fluent bureaucratise, Walcott added, "It remains to be manifested, what will be the effect of law assistance in the Kentucky survey . . . but it has been confidently expected that it would produce material consequences, not only upon the revenue of the year now current, but in regard to the arrears due, for the two preceding."[46]

On the local scene, communications from Morrison and his revenue collector, John Arthur, also testify to the continued procrastination. Morrison informed the distillers, "From the positive instructions I have lately received from the commissioner of the revenue [Tench Coxe] to have the duties now due, collected with the greatest promptitude, and transmitted to the treasury of the United States, it will be entirely out of my power to give longer indulgence to delinquent distillers."[47] Arthur's communique advised the distillers that the law required that "all stills must be entered in June annually, whether for use or otherwise.—It is therefore expected, the distillers will comply, and not subject themselves to the penalty incurred for non-entrance."[48] Almost four years after its formation, the Ohio District was included for the first time in revenue returns for the year ending June 30, 1798. Collections on distilled spirits and stills for this heretofore unproductive district amounted to $38,234 out of a total of $520,101 for the entire United States.[49]

In addition to laying down guidelines, the federal government was taking legal action. The wording of typical indictments is highly suggestive of the statewide inattention to bureaucratic supervision: "for using two stills and worms in the distillation of spirits . . . contrary to . . . Act of Congress"; "three stills

---

[46] U.S., *American State Papers, Finance*, 1:558. The above and succeeding revenue figures in this chapter are rounded off to the nearest dollar.

[47] *Gazette*, June 13, 1798.

[48] Ibid. Revenue Collector Arthur was also the owner of a store and bought quantities of whiskey. See ibid., December 26, 1798.

[49] U.S., *American State Papers, Finance*, 1:621.

and not entering them"; "being possessed of a still, failed to enter her."[50] District court proceedings for several years were devoted to clearing up the backlog of cases against the first "moonshiners" of Kentucky. Willard R. Jillson lists 177 cases of this kind, for infractions in the period from June 15, 1794, to June 30, 1800. The distillers of twenty-one counties are represented, and the assessed United States debts ranged from $16.91 to $637.66½ per person.[51] One famous casualty of this action was the Reverend Elijah Craig of Scott County, whose liability was established at $140.00. Craig obviously had financial difficulties during the latter years of his life, as indicated by a letter of 1800: "I have bin unsucsesfull, in a measure, in persutes valuable for My Country, so that I cannot now pay even my federal Tax without distressing my family."[52]

The repeal of the hated excise was foreshadowed when the Federalists failed in the election of 1800, although the official enactment was not effective until June 30, 1802.[53] When this news reached Kentucky, it was hailed with rapture:

Jubilee Wednesday last, 30th June, the internal duties on stills and domestic distilled spirits, on refined sugars, licenses to retailers, sales at auction, carriages for the conveyance of persons, and stamped vellum, parchment and paper ceased. The citizens of Kentucky felt indignation on the passage of the laws laying those duties—they experienced the baneful effects of their operation, (particularly the excise and stamp laws) and they rejoiced in their repeal.—In the evening the Lexington Light Infantry

[50] Memorandum by Innes, July 1779, Innes Papers, fol. 27, part 1, 87; June 1800, fol. 27, part 2, 174; U.S., District Court Records, Kentucky District, 1789–1800, section 1, 51, 128; section 2, 1, 44–48; U.S. District Court Order Book, Kentucky District, 1795–1801, 46.

[51] Willard Rouse Jillson, *Early Kentucky Distillers, 1783–1800* (Louisville, 1940), 44–49. There is actually a total of 173 distillers, by name; four are named twice. This work does not contain records of any distillers from Jefferson and several other counties in existence at the time. Of the twenty-one counties listed by Jillson, Scott led the list with thirty delinquents, and Bourbon was second with twenty-three.

[52] Lyman C. Draper Manuscripts, State Historical Society of Wisconsin, 5 CC 3. For Craig's fine, see Jillson, *Early Kentucky Distillers*, 46.

[53] U.S., *Statutes at Large*, 2:148–50.

paraded and fired seventeen vollies of muquetry [sic]—the bell rang a joyful peal—the bonfires blazed—shouts rent the air &c. In due time the citizens retired to their respective homes in perfect harmony.[54]

On the following fourth of July, one of the many toasts drunk in honor of the occasion was to "public oeconomy—may it supercede the necessity of that detestable British system of finance, called excise, and stamp-laws."[55]

More soberly, Mann Butler's account of the repeal explains some of the reasons why the distillers had hated the tax, and their suspicion of its political purpose: "The repeal of the internal taxes relieved our interior agricultural country, ill able to command specie, from much irritating interference of excise officers: whose salaries in an extensive country like this Union, form a great drawback from the product of such taxes to the national treasury, and contributed much, to augment the patronage and influence of the Federal Executive."[56]

Eleven and a half years later, another period of national financial stress was sufficiently pressing to require a whiskey tax. This was during the latter stages of the War of 1812, and lasted from January 1, 1814, to the end of 1817. News of the proposed second excise, as reported in the Lexington press, reflected both apprehension and suspicion:

. . . the bill levying an Excise Tax, has been discussed: The following extract of a letter will shew the temper of the house on this subject, which does not auger well: "A proposition was made to strike out the provision laying 108 cents per gallon on the capacity of the still, and rateably, to make way to lay a tax on the quantity distilled, say 25 cents per gallon—It failed only by *one* vote, & will, it is said, be again brought forward. If it succeeds much delay will take place, much injustice be done, and it may be the system will fall. The eastern people seem to wish

[54] *Gazette*, July 2, 1802.
[55] Ibid., July 9, 1802.
[56] Mann Butler, *A History of the Commonwealth of Kentucky* (Louisville, 1834), 299.

Whiskey to bear the whole burthen of the war and be a substitute at least for the land tax."[57]

In some respects the second excise was similar to the first. For distilling spirits from domestic materials, and before the start of operations, a license was required. Charges for this permit were based on graduated rates for seven periods of use, ranging from nine cents per gallon of capacity for a two-week period, to one hundred and eight cents per gallon for the entire year. An important difference from the former excise was the imposition of a special tax on boilers in distilleries using steam to heat the mash—rates for boiler capacity were double that required of stills.[58] Modifications to this enactment, effective February 1, 1815, provided for an additional twenty cents per gallon on all spirits distilled from domestic materials. An option was included for the owners of stills with capacity not exceeding 100 gallons, or boilers not exceeding 50 gallons; this allowed the payment of twenty-five cents for every gallon of spirits distilled, in lieu of the other provisions.[59]

To judge from the lack of published complaint, the new excise was evaded far less than had been the first. A few distillers, however, must have persisted in their deplorable ways, for in 1817 they were reminded:

Notice is hereby given, that all bonds due by Distillers for duties on stills that may remain unpaid in my office on the last day of this month, will be immediately thereafter (without discrimination) handed over to the Attorney for the U.S. to put in suit.[60]

By this time far fewer distillers could plead ignorance as their excuse, for the number of local newspapers had increased, giving governmental requirements much wider publicity than would have been possible in the 1790s.[61] There was also evident, on the

[57] *Gazette*, July 13, 1813.
[58] U.S., *Statutes at Large*, 3:42–44.
[59] Ibid., 152–59.
[60] *Gazette*, September 6, 1817.
[61] See, for example, ibid., September 7, 1813; January 2, 1815; April 8,

part of the tax authorities, a somewhat more realistic approach to the facts of western life, as shown by a notice the Treasury Department issued to its local collectors:

To guard against the misapprehensions that may arise, in regard to the descriptions of money demandable for the internal duties and direct tax, it is considered proper to advise you that the revenue will not be collected in coin on the first of October next, unless an arrangement shall be effected with the State Banks to supply the community with the necessary medium, and that due notice will be given of such an arrangement, if made.[62]

Treasury Department returns for the four-year period (1814–1817) reflect an improved administration of the second excise in Kentucky, as compared with the earlier one. For the duties on still and boiler licenses issued within the state, receipts amounted to $384,325. Also collected was $196,725 for the additional twenty-cent per gallon tax, and $65,027 for the optional tax which concerned owners of single stills with capacity less than 100 gallons.[63] The second excise tax ended on December 31, 1817, and was the last whiskey tax until the onset of the Civil War.[64]

There is room to doubt that either of the tax periods was as financially burdensome as the laments of the distillers would indicate. Prices current, as reported in the Lexington *Gazette*, show that minimum whiskey quotations averaged several cents per gallon higher toward the end of the first excise (in both Natchez and New Orleans) than in the four years immediately following its repeal.[65] Figures from the same source disclose that whiskey prices during the second excise were ten to fifteen cents

1816; January 10, 1818; *Correspondent*, February 6, 1815; *Patriot*, April 20, June 8, 1816; *Lexington Western Monitor*, January 20, February 10, March 24, 1815; hereafter cited as *Western Monitor*.

[62] *Patriot*, September 14, 1816.

[63] All revenue returns from U.S., *American State Papers, Finance*, 3:51, 207, 216, 298.

[64] U.S., *Statutes at Large*, 3:401–03.

[65] *Gazette*, September 1, 1800, to July 22, 1806.

higher than those of the years immediately preceding, and twenty to forty cents higher than in the three years following. Quotations covering in-state sales for the same period show a range of fifteen to thirty-three cents greater during the tax years than either before or after.[66] Thus it would appear that the hard-pressed distillers did not add to their difficulties by completely absorbing the tax charges. The largest distilling project of the entire period was commenced during the second excise, at a time when the secretary of the treasury was recommending that the liquor tax be retained on a permanent basis.[67]

[66] Ibid., January 15, 1811, to September 7, 1820.

[67] U.S., *American State Papers*, *Finance*, 3:16–17. Secretary Dallas proposed on December 6, 1815, to discontinue the duties on distilled spirits after June 30, 1816; the duty on licenses to distillers was to be raised at that time to double the amount fixed by the enactment of July 24, 1813. Ibid. See chapter 3 above, pp. 57–58, for a discussion of the Hope Distillery.

6

Whiskey of Distinction

A s w e h a v e s e e n, the first half-century of Kentucky distilling brought improvements in basic equipment—greater
still capacity, the steam process, condensing chambers—all tending to increase the volume of production with a greater degree of
efficiency. At about the same time there were numerous other
developments in technique and a somewhat more sophisticated
approach to advertising and marketing. Whiskey was becoming
better and better. The genesis of a distinctive regional distillate—
bourbon whiskey—was apparent for some time before the product
acquired its name.

To some extent, expediency had governed the initial phase of
whiskey production in Kentucky, as it had in the older settlements.
Commercially speaking, two classes of consumers furnished the
distiller's clientele during this period—frontiersmen and Indians.
Neither group was noted for discrimination or fastidiousness in
its drinking habits. Shortly before the beginning of the nineteenth
century, however, some changes became apparent, both in the
consumers and in the quality of their whiskey. Flourishing thirsty
communities replaced the thirsty frontier society. Increasingly,
people paid money for their whiskey instead of bartering farm
produce for it, and they demanded better quality.

One of the first indications that distillers were heeding the
demand was a growing emphasis on the proof content of the

product. Historically, the term "proof" was used to signify the approximate alcoholic content of distilled spirits; "proof spirits" were considered as containing equal parts of water and alcohol.[1] Before the hydrometer came into general use, distillers employed several crude methods for ascertaining the approximate ratio. One method, of ancient origin and universal use, involved the use of gunpowder and logically led to the designation of spirits as "bearing Proof of Gunpowder."[2] As implied by this descriptive terminology, the strength of spirits was determined (proved) "by pouring it into a dish containing gunpowder and inflaming it: if it took fire, it was said that the spirit was *above* proof; if not, it was *under* or *below* proof."[3] Harrison Hall was somewhat more graphic in his explanation of the same principle: "Pour a small quantity of spirit on a small heap of gunpowder and kindle it. The spirit burns quietly on the surface of the powder until it is all consumed, and the last portion fires the powder if the spirit was pure, but if watery, the powder becomes too damp and will not explode."[4] Obviously, such a procedure contributed to the fire hazard in distilling operations, and contemporary texts on distilling caution distillers to "beware of lighted candles, torches, papers, or other combustible matter being brought too near your still."[5]

Another method, equally crude, was described by George Smith in 1738: "To get proof goods: small quantity in glass Phyal, shake it, if the blebs or proof of it continues a pretty while upon the top or surface of the goods, it is then what is called proof-

[1] Harrison Hall, *The Distiller* (Philadelphia, 1818), 261; Peter Jonas, *A Complete Set of New Hydrometer Tables* (London, 1807), vi.

[2] W. Y——Worth, *Dr. Worth's Letter in Answer to W. R. Gent* (London, 1691), 118.

[3] Lewis Feuchtwanger, *Fermented Liquors: A Treatise on Brewing, Distilling, Rectifying, and Manufacturing of Sugars, Wines, Spirits* . . . (New York, 1858), 70.

[4] Hall, *Distiller*, 263.

[5] George Smith, *A Compleat Body of Distilling* . . . (London, 1738), 76; regarding the fire hazard, see also A. Cooper, *The Complete Distiller* (London, 1757), 43–44; Hall, *Distiller*, 261.

goods. . . . Below proof: upon your shaking the Phyal or glass, the goods will fall flat, or the blebs or proof thereof will not continue on the surface of it."[6] Other works on distilling of about the same time mention "bubble proof" as the general criterion of spirits and undoubtedly refer to this method. Many distillers of illegal whiskey and brandy in modern times resort to this very means of obtaining a rough and quick approximation of the alcoholic content of their products. There is a slight variation in nomenclature; "blebs" become "bead" in modern parlance.

Various other hit-or-miss methods of proofing were in use before the complete acceptance of instruments and were probably about as reliable as the procedures just described. In 1787 the Davidson County (Tennessee) court alluded to one frontier means of proofing when it established tavern rates for "½ pint whisky such as will sink tallow 2 shillings."[7] In 1796 the Lexington *Gazette* published "infallible and simple" instructions for "all purchasers of distilled spirits, who do not know how to prove the strength of them": "Take half a pint of spirits in a cup or tumbler, take a small quantity of clean cotton, lay it as light as possible on the surface of the liquor; if your spirits be good proof, the cotton will sink immediately to the bottom; add a little water to it and the cotton will rise."[8]

Toward the end of the eighteenth century there began to appear evidence of considerable use of the so-called "philosophic instruments" in determining the proof of distilled spirits. More than any other method, this had the practical effect of initiating the use of a standard proofing terminology. Most of the hydrometers and thermometers manufactured in this country were made in Philadelphia. A typical advertisement in the *Pennsylvania Packet* advised the public in 1789 that the subscriber made and sold "the best Barometers, Thermometers, and Glass Bubbles to prove

[6] Smith, *Compleat Body*, 70.
[7] Quoted in Elsie Lathrop, *Early American Inns and Taverns* (New York, 1936), 300.
[8] *Gazette*, July 16, 1796.

spirits, of different kinds."[9] England was the customary source of foreign-made hydrometers; in 1791 the "Dycas's patent Hydrometers complete" cost three and a half guineas in London.[10]

Certainly the most influential force in defining a uniform system of proofing and in requiring the use of proofing instruments on all distilled products was the Excise Act of 1791. The terms of this enactment specified six different proofs for spirits "distilled within the United States, from any article of the growth or produce of the United States." The officially-designated standard of measurement for the forthcoming adventure in bureaucracy was "Dicas's hydrometer."[11] It was further provided "that it be the duty of the Secretary of the Treasury to provide and furnish to the officers of inspection and of the customs, proper instruments for ascertaining the said several proofs."[12] The estimated cost of hydrometers for the use of customs and revenue officials, for the year 1792, was one thousand dollars.[13]

The growing use of instruments for determining the proof content in distilled spirits during the first two decades of the nineteenth century is confirmed by advertisements which featured "hydrometers," "a good set of Guaging [sic] instruments," and the like.[14] Several works on distilling were published about this time; without exception, they stressed the value of thermometers and hydrometers. Hall, for example, thought that these devices "should always be at hand, and frequently resorted to."[15] Boucherie considered the "Areometer, or Proof Bottle," to be of such importance that a whole chapter of his treatise was devoted to its

[9] Quoted in Harrold E. Gillingham, "Some Early Philadelphia Instrument Makers," *Pennsylvania Magazine of History and Biography* 51 (1927):305; see also ibid., 306; *Evening Herald*, February 10, March 17, 1787.

[10] Harold C. Syrett, ed., *The Papers of Alexander Hamilton* (in progress; New York, 1961–), 8:542.

[11] U.S., *Statutes at Large*, 1:203.

[12] Ibid., 208.

[13] Syrett, *Papers of Alexander Hamilton*, 9:466, 475.

[14] *Gazette*, April 11, 1814; November 8, 1817; August 27, 1819.

[15] Hall, *Distiller*, 227.

use. "This instrument is indispensable to the distiller: it ascertains the value of his spirits, since it shows the result of their degrees of concentration. . . . The areometer can only be just, when the atmosphere is temperate; that is, at 55° Farenheit."[16]

With the official adoption of federal guidelines for defining the alcoholic content of spirits, there followed a definite increase in the use of "proof" as a commercial standard of quality in Kentucky whiskey. Advertisements of both whiskey and brandy, heretofore rarely distinguished by descriptive allusions to actual content, shortly began to include designations of quality such as "full proof," "good proof," and "well tested."[17] In order to more fully describe their products in 1825, the Union Mills of Lexington categorized their whiskey as "fifth proof and common proof."[18] Additional federal influence in this direction was provided by the periodic notices from the War Department's Office of Commissary General which solicited bids for the supply of rations at widely scattered military establishments. The maintenance of national security in those perilous times required truly staggering quantities of whiskey, and this was characteristically designated as "proof whiskey" or "good proof whiskey."[19] The annual military requirements at times exceeded 120,000 gallons; thus the tendency toward a standardized nomenclature affected the operations of a great many distillers, in Kentucky and elsewhere.

Along with this emphasis on alcoholic content went an increasing devotion to "age" as a criterion of quality. This reverence was not unanimous, to judge from Ebenezer Stedman's account of his experiences in the Georgetown area: "I went to the still house that

[16] Anthony Boucherie, *The Art of Making Whiskey* (Lexington, Kentucky, 1819), 33–34.

[17] *Gazette*, March 8, 1797; February 28, 1804; October 11, 1808; November 16, 1820.

[18] Ibid., November 18, 1825. Fifth proof referred to "spirits more than twenty and not more than forty per cent above proof." U.S., *Statutes at Large*, 1:203, 208.

[19] *Gazette*, August 20, 1819; August 31, 1820; August 16, 1821; August 22, 1822; August 5, 1824.

Stood oposite webbs house For a gallon of Whiskey that was, as Col Cox usto Say, a weak old lacking Five Days."[20] Nevertheless, the advertisements of the period reflect a growing respect for the proper aging of whiskey and brandy. A Mercer County distiller advertised in 1793 that he had five hundred gallons of "Old Whiskey" for sale.[21] The customers were also becoming aware of the blessings of senectitude, as is apparent in the notice of a Lexington firm in 1794; William Morton indicated that he was in the market for "a quantity of old Peach Brandy."[22]

"Old whiskey" was widely advertised during the first quarter of the nineteenth century.[23] Popular taste was improving and the distillers and merchants of spirits were catering to it. Even the aging of whiskey on its way to market was recognized and counted in its favor. One writer, referring to the distillers of Kentucky and Tennessee, remarked: "As they depend upon the rise of the rivers to send their whiskey to market, it acquires some age: this also, and the motion of travelling, has considerable effect in improving it."[24]

In some areas of Kentucky the merchants began to distinguish in their advertising between "common" (or "new") and "old" whiskey. In 1814 the Mauray firm of Louisville advised the public of both "old" and "common" in their description of rye whiskey.[25] M. J. Nouvel of Lexington announced in 1820 that he had "a few Barrels of very superior Old Whiskey, By the Barrel or Gallon—Also, Good New Whiskey, By the Barrel."[26] Nouvel's

[20] Frances L. S. Dugan and Jacqueline P. Bull, eds., *Bluegrass Craftsman: Being the Reminiscences of Ebenezer Hiram Stedman, Papermaker, 1808–1885* (Lexington, 1959), 45. Stedman's approach to the age factor was pragmatic rather than consistent. On other occasions he showed an appreciation for properly aged whiskey.

[21] *Gazette*, September 28, 1793.

[22] Ibid., October 11, 1794.

[23] See, for example, *Gazette*, October 4, 1808; *Correspondent*, July 6, 1814; *Western Herald*, July 6, 1825; *Western Citizen*, January 21, 1826; *Olive Branch*, September 29, 1826; *Commentator*, June 14, 1828.

[24] Hall, *Distiller*, 15.

[25] *Correspondent*, October 19, 1814.

[26] *Gazette*, March 10, 1820.

apparent willingness to sell the better product by the gallon is undoubtedly a reflection of local consumer preference. In 1825, Peter Wickham of Bardstown advertised "from 80 to 90 barrels of first rate new and old whiskey for sale."[27]

The definitive description of whiskey age, in terms of actual years, began to appear at about the same time. In 1814, Elijah Noble notified prospective customers that he had, for sale, "100 barrels two years old WHISKEY."[28] Four years later, the Lexington *Gazette* carried its first specific reference to whiskey age (in terms of years) when it published John Stickney's notice of seven-year-old whiskey for sale.[29] In the following year (1819) Stickney modified his claim slightly by advertising "Whiskey at 9s per gal., said to be 7 years old."[30] Judging from several examples of concurrent whiskey prices, this quotation represented unbounded confidence in the advantages accruing from the aging process. The same issue of the *Gazette* carried an extract of a letter from New Orleans which quoted whiskey (as of March 1, 1819) at fifty cents per gallon. The Panic of 1819 was getting under way at this time, and during the following two years the price of whiskey at New Orleans was to reach a low of nineteen cents.[31]

The improvement in whiskey contributed materially to the pursuit of happiness in early Kentucky, as recorded in Ebenezer Stedman's rapturous account of a fishing excursion: "Such a fine time we had that night in fishing and drinking That old whiskey. It was Made in 1822 and Sold to Michal Barton in frankfort at 25 cents per gallon and this was in 1835. So it was 11 years old [*sic*], and pure and a man Could not get drunk on that whiskey in a day."[32] Stedman's unbounded confidence in "That old whiskey" was indicative of a general trend at that time. Increasing

[27] *Western Herald*, July 6, 1825.
[28] *Western Monitor*, September 23, 1814.
[29] *Gazette*, November 6, 1818.
[30] Ibid., March 26, 1819.
[31] Ibid., July 12, 1821.
[32] Dugan and Bull, *Bluegrass Craftsman*, 184.

respect for age in whiskey was evident also in the wine list of Lexington's Phoenix Hotel, publicized in 1834, which proclaimed, as an inducement to convivial-minded patrons, that ten-year-old Irish whiskey would be regularly stocked in the hotel's bar and cellar. Significantly, there was no mention of the product which later made the area famous.[33]

Changes were also apparent in the construction of still-houses. In this there was room for improvement, for in all likelihood the earlier still-houses were similar to the one built by General John Burrows, a Pennsylvania distiller of the 1790s. Burrows merely "dug a place in the bank, along-side of a well, and put up a small log still-house."[34] The establishments of the early Kentucky distillers were of much the same sort, though the Kentuckians normally depended on streams and springs for their water supply. Before the end of the century, however, they were building still-houses of more permanent construction and locating them with more regard for operational efficiency.

Both the transient nature of early distilling and its subsequent evolvement into permanent distilleries are illustrated by approximately three decades of advertisements in the Lexington *Gazette*. At first the references were only to the basic equipment—stills and worms. In the early 1790s, however, the term "distillery" came into use to describe the entire installation.[35] By 1794, a Scott County resident included in his description of property for sale, a distillery, "the conveniences of which is equal to any in this State."[36] A Madison County notice of 1799 emphasized one of the essential features of permanent installations in a description which included "sufficient water to drive two pair of stones during the greatest drought in Summer. There is likewise an excellent seat for a Distillery, with overhead water—a house built for that

[33] *Gazette*, January 18, 1834.
[34] "Autobiographical Sketch of the Life of General John Burrows, of Lycoming Co., Penna.," *Pennsylvania Magazine of History and Biography* 34 (1910):429.
[35] *Gazette*, June 25, August 18, 1791.
[36] Ibid., February 22, 1794.

purpose, thirty feet by twenty."[37] In Jessamine County a farm was offered for rent (1801) which included "a distillery, 60 × 34 ft. with stills and boilers for a house of that size."[38]

Shortly after the turn of the century, still-houses of a more substantial nature were in evidence; the common distinguishing feature was construction of stone. Within seven miles of Lexington, "a stone still-house, 30 feet by 20" was offered for sale in 1805.[39] Four years later there were featured, in the same advertisement, three stone distilleries for sale by the quondam state senator, Peyton Short (1792–1796); two were described simply as "large," and the third as "handsome and convenient."[40] A Fayette County farm of seventy-two acres included "a good stone still house, forty feet long, 26 wide, with three stills and every thing necessary for making whiskey."[41] The existence and frequency of these and similar advertisements conclusively illustrate the transition to distilling as a full-time, year-round business.

It can be assumed that the distilleries described in newspaper advertisements represent only a minor portion of the total number in existence during the period. Nor was the construction of permanent-type buildings limited to Fayette County. For example, the Georgetown *Patriot* of 1816 listed a lot in the town for sale and included the following information: "There is built on the lot a stone house for a distillery supplied with water from a lasting spring, conveyed in pipes giving 13 feet head."[42] In Louisville, the short-lived Hope Distillery enterprise was typical of this building trend.

The change in architecture was, to some extent, symbolic, for it was accompanied by further changes in distilling itself—all addressed toward greater volume and efficiency of production and convenience of marketing. In Russell County, the former

[37] Ibid., February 14, 1799.
[38] Ibid., December 4, 1801.
[39] Ibid., January 22, 1805.
[40] Ibid., January 3, 1809.
[41] Ibid., April 3, 1810.
[42] *Patriot*, May 26, 1816.

property of the Honorable B. Y. Owsley featured a 1,200-acre farm which included:

A Large Brick Steam Distillery, capable of making 3 Barrels of Whisky per day, the whole year. There is an abundance of Cold Spring Water to run the Distillery the driest time ever known in Kentucky; and a ready market, at a fair price, for all the Whisky that can possibly be made. And there is perhaps no place in Kentucky where CORN can be produced as cheap, and as conveniently for a Distillery, as at this point, the River [Cumberland] affording ample facilities for the transportation of both Corn and Whisky. Steamboats pass the property from six to eight months in the year.[43]

Similar features characterized a Franklin County distillery, one mile below Frankfort on the Kentucky River:

. . . has an excellent wharf perfectly convenient for the landing of coal, wood, grain, etc., and equally so for the shipping of everything either up or down the river. The improvements consist of a large three story stone warehouse, a still-house, woodhouse, and excellent pens. The machinery is of the best and most approved patterns for making copper distilled Whisky, the engine is a splendid one and entirely new, having cost a few months since, one thousand dollars. The establishment is supplied by a splendid spring of pure water which never fails and never gets muddy.[44]

As might be expected, the more businesslike approach to distilling brought improvements in industrial sanitation, particularly insofar as it affected the quality of the product. Herein one must assume the pioneer distiller had often been deplorably careless; now there was less and less excuse. Many treatises on distilling in this and earlier periods stressed both cleanliness and efficiency in distilling operations. As early as 1738, one of these had advised prospective distillers to pave the still-house floor with wide

---

[43] *Western Citizen*, March 12, 1852. B. Y. Owsley was U.S. representative from Kentucky, 1841–1843; Richard H. Collins *History of Kentucky* (Covington, 1874), 1:352.

[44] *Western Citizen*, October 8, 1858.

stones and include sufficient pitch in the floor to carry off wash from the still, as well as occasional slop, "whereby your Still-house floor will always be clean."[45] For the mashing operation, Michael Krafft emphasized that the vessels be "well scalded and aired."[46] Jonathan Taylor considered the personal traits of distillery personnel sufficiently important to include this admonition: "In the first place the distiller must be an industrious man a cleanly sober watchfull man."[47]

The pay of such exemplary employees was surprisingly good. In 1807, for example, it was possible for capable distillers to earn forty dollars per month.[48] Harrison Hall estimated, in 1818, distiller wages of "one dollar per day for the best hands" or four to five cents per gallon on the quantity distilled.[49]

For a brief span of years, there was an unusual amount of local promotional activity for Kentucky whiskey. This took the form of exhibits in agricultural fairs for which premiums were annually awarded to the best locally produced samples. Perhaps to a greater extent than any other evidence, this serves to illustrate how thoroughly distilling was accepted in early Kentucky society. In addition, the importance of whiskey in the economy of the state is verified by its choice as one of the competing domestic products; in the first fair held within Kentucky, whiskey was one of only five general classifications of entries.

At the first fair in Fayette County, held in 1814 and lasting for three days, a total of twenty-three silver cups were awarded. Livestock competition accounted for fifteen of the awards, five were for home-manufactured cloth of different kinds, and one cup each was presented for the best entry of wheat, cheese, and whiskey. Specifications for the whiskey entrants provided that a silver

[45] Smith, *Compleat Body*, 60.
[46] Michael August Krafft, *The American Distiller* (Philadelphia, 1804), 68.
[47] Jonathan Taylor, Manuscript Diary, 1774–1815(?), Filson Club, Louisville, Kentucky.
[48] *Gazette*, December 29, 1807.
[49] Hall, *Distiller*, 31.

cup be awarded "to the best whisky, not less than one hundred gallons, of this year's make."[50]

In March of 1817, the Kentucky Agricultural Society met and "voted premiums for the next Fair." Their stipulated awards included a silver cup "to the distiller who shall make 100 gallons of the best Whisky, a specimen, with satisfactory certificates, and to be produced."[51] When the results of this competition were published in the following June, Melchor Hoover was listed as winner of the whiskey premium.[52] It is evident from the wording of the award specifications that an attempt was being made to favor competition from bona fide distillers only.

In June of 1818, Robert Crockett was recipient of a premium for the best sample of whiskey, "with satisfactory assurances of . . . having 100 gallons more made in the preceeding season."[53] Whiskey competition for 1819 had been expanded to include the Cattle Show in June and the annual meeting in September. At the latter, Robert Crockett was again awarded a silver cup; his "sample of excellent Whiskey" was thought superior for both strength and flavor.[54] On the same occasion, the admirable Crockett was announced as fourth vice president and member of the Corresponding Committee and Committee of Arrangements for the ensuing year.

In 1821 the Bourbon Agricultural Society announced that its exhibitions for that year would be held at the farm of Colonel Henry Clay, two miles from Paris on the road to Winchester. Showing considerably more ambition in their approach, or profiting from the Fayette County examples of the preceding years, the committee offered the customary premium of a silver cup to "The best Whiskey: a sample of one quart to be exhibited, and the distiller giving to the society satisfactory evidence of having,

[50] George W. Ranck, *History of Lexington, Kentucky* (Cincinnati, 1872), 271–72; William Henry Perrin, ed., *History of Fayette County, Kentucky* (Chicago, 1882), 119–20.
[51] *Gazette*, March 31, 1817.
[52] Ibid., June 16, 1817.
[53] Ibid., March 13, June 26, 1818.
[54] Ibid., May 7, June 18, October 8, 1819.

during the last distilling season, manufactured at least one thousand gallons of equal quality."[55] This requirement would have effectively limited competition to those making a business out of whiskey production.

It is unfortunate for distilling history that the beginning practice of whiskey competition at agricultural fairs coincided in time and space with the equally incipient temperance movement in Kentucky. There is no other adequate explanation for the abrupt cessation of whiskey publicity at these events. The local temperance movement was well under way by the time of the Franklin County Agricultural Fair in 1836; advance publicity omitted the customary reference to whiskey exhibits and specified that booths and stalls for the sale of spirituous liquors were expressly prohibited.[56] The omission of whiskey exhibits at agricultural fairs was not peculiar to Franklin County; for example, at the fairs of Bourbon, Woodford, and Fayette counties during the late 1830s, there were no advertised premiums for whiskey.[57]

Through the late eighteenth century, there seems to have been little effort to standardize the proportion of grains used in distilling; to the frontier distiller, such a refinement would hardly have been possible. He used whatever grain was available. One recipe, dating from the turn of the century, advises: "Mash one bushel and a half in each tubb if you have rye to mix put the corn in first and to every bushel of corn make use of 24 gallons of scalding water let it stand covered up an hour then put in the malt. . . . let it stand so for 20 minutes then stir it up and put in the rye meal."[58]

By the third decade of the nineteenth century, however, a change could be noted. The first complete recipe appearing in the Lexington *Gazette* was published in 1823 and quoted a locally published pamphlet, "A Receipt for distilling by a process

[55] Ibid., September 20, 1821.

[56] *Argus*, April 27, 1836.

[57] *Western Citizen*, July 19, 1839; *Argus*, July 28, 1837; *Gazette*, July 25, 1835.

[58] Taylor, Diary.

called the sweet mash, by which an average of two gallons of excellent spirit has been made by a noted distiller in the neighborhood of Lexington":

Pour twelve gallons of boiling water into an hundred gallon tub, add one handful of hops, then half a bushel of corn-meal, stir the contents well, again pour in twelve gallons of boiling water and half bushel of meal, repeating the stirring to prevent the meal from collecting into lumps. Then pour in twelve gallons more of water and another half bushel of meal, and stir again; let it stand until so cool, the distiller can bear his hand four inches within the surface of the mash, with out more pain than a slight stinging sensation at the ends of his fingers. Then put in a half a gallon of malt and four gallons of rye or wheat meal, after which, stir the vessel about half way, to the bottom, so as to weyt the meal, and let it stand ten minutes; then stir down to the bottom, and repeat the stirring every ten minutes until the liquor shall be about milk-warm, or until you can insert your hand into it nine inches without pain. Fill up the tub within four or five inches of the top with cold or cool water, then add half a gallon of yest, and if the weather be very cold, the tub may be covered over with a mat for one night. The tub is then suffered to stand until the bubbles cease to rise, then it will be ready for distillation; and after being well stirred up, the beer should be poured into the still for distillation.[59]

The grain proportions of this concoction are remarkably similar to some that were being used almost a century and a half later in the production of bourbon whiskey.

The same issue of the *Gazette* carried "A Receipt for making three gallons of spirit from a bushel of grain, successfully practiced in Fayette County":

Pour into a one hundred gallon tub twelve gallons of still-slop to each tub, half a bushel of corn meal, twelve gallons of slop, half bushel of meal and again the same, each time well stirred. Let it stand in cool weather two days, in warm one and a half days, add a half-gallon of malt, and two gallons of warm water,

[59] *Gazette*, November 27, 1823.

and half a gallon of rye meal, and one gallon of yest; after standing fifteen minutes stir it in at the top, then fill up the tub within a few inches of the top, with water; in winter cover it with a mat one night, in warm weather it does not require a covering, it stands then until it quits blubbering when it will be fit for distillation. The sweet mash should be resorted to every fourth operation, because after repeated distillation, the slop becomes fiery and disagreeable. By this mode three and a fourth gallons of good spirit have been made to the bushel of grain, and an average, of two and a half gallons during a whole stilling season. Whilst practising this process great care should be taken to keep the tubs clean, as they are very apt to sour and in that case the liquor is injured.[60]

In 1833 the Lexington distillery of Daniel and Henry McCourt notified the public that they wanted "Corn, Rye and Barley, for which the highest market price will be given in cash—to be delivered at the Distillery formerly occupied by Mr. Benajah Bosworth, one mile from the city, convenient to the Railroad. N. B. Yellow Corn would be preferred."[61] It is evident from this example, as well as the foregoing recipes, that standardization was increasing in both the selection of raw materials and the respective grain percentages used in mashing.

Judging from the many earlier references to whiskey manufactured from corn, or from combinations of corn with smaller grains, it becomes obvious that the mixture antedated the name which was later applied to such distillates. Forms of corn whiskey had been manufactured in America as early as 1682 and were continuously made from that time until the distinctive name "bourbon" became an accepted type-description. Various combinations were reminiscent of the proportions for modern bourbon whiskey; with but few minor adjustments, the two immediately preceding recipes could be used satisfactorily. The Hope Distillery notices of grains desired (chapter 3) reflect the proportions used

[60] Ibid. While not identified as such, this recipe would produce a "sour mash" type of whiskey.
[61] Ibid., April 13, 1833.

119

in present-day bourbon, as do those of the Lexington distillery, above.

Within a period of approximately twenty-five years, distinctive names as applied to whiskey types achieved a certain amount of recognition and local usage. By 1817, for example, Kentucky grocery stores began to feature "Irish Whiskey" in their assortment of liquors for sale.[62] This was a time, however, of frontier enterprise and free emulation of foreign products, and it may be safely assumed that a goodly portion of this "Irish" whiskey was locally produced. Many advertisements and treatises on distilling contained undisguised instructions for making not only Irish whiskey but Monongahela rye, Holland gin, brandy, Jamaica spirits, and even bourbon whiskey.[63] This was not the immediate case with the first bourbon, for it was of local extraction; several years were to elapse before it achieved sufficient renown to justify imitation. By the early 1830s Old Monongahela rye whiskey was being widely advertised in the Kentucky area, and the same was true of Old Scotch some ten years later—both types could well have represented imitations.[64]

The first known advertisement featuring the distinctive Kentucky product appeared, and fittingly so, in a Bourbon County newspaper for 1821. The Maysville firm of Stout and Adams used the *Western Citizen* to publicize "BOURBON WHISKEY" by the barrel or keg.[65] The use of this nomenclature was to remain almost completely local for the next several years, but by 1840 the use of "bourbon" in identifying this delightful whiskey had become a statewide practice. In Lexington, Ben Crutchfield's

[62] Ibid., October 11, 1817.

[63] See, for example, ibid., March 12, 1805; November 27, 1823; March 15, 1834; Krafft, *American Distiller*, 161; Boucherie, *Art of Making Whiskey*, 39; Feuchtwanger, *Fermented Liquors*, 87–88.

[64] In Louisville, "Old Monongahela Whiskey" was being offered in fifty-barrel lots by Starkey and Gwathmey, Grocers. See *Louisville Daily Journal*, November 26, 1830; cited hereafter as *Daily Journal*. See also *Gazette*, March 8, June 21, 1834; *Western Citizen*, October 24, 1845. The same whiskey was advertised by Cincinnati grocery stores as early as 1822; see *Cincinnati Inquisitor and Cincinnati Advertiser*, May 7, 1822.

[65] *Western Citizen*, June 26, 1821.

grocery store, located on Main Street, published the most comprehensive listing (to date) of wines and liquors available in the Bluegrass. Included in the latter group, and attesting to the status recently achieved by the Kentucky product, were Cognac Brandy, Jamaica Spirits, Holland Gin, Irish and Old Bourbon Whiskey.[66] Similar advertising campaigns were conducted by the merchants of Louisville and other cities through the use of newspapers in smaller localities.[67] A Cincinnati business house, specializing in fancy groceries, offered "Holland Gin, Jamaica and St. Croix Rum, superior Old Scotch and Irish Whiskey, Old Bourbon and Monongahela Whiskey, and fine Old Gin, imported in jugs and cans."[68]

As we have seen, the first fifty years of distilling in Kentucky brought about great improvements, both in production methods and in the finished product. One logical development remained to complete the picture—the public identification of individual distillers with their whiskey and the competitive quality of that whiskey. Consumers preferred to identify and purchase those makes of whiskey they could drink with confidence. Evidence of "name" whiskey is noticeable in the newspapers of the 1820s, witnessing the growth of local reputations of deserving distillers; it was to be a continuing factor in whiskey advertisements and sales until the formal use of brands, which came several years later. One of the first notices to publicly identify the makers with an implied quality in their product appeared in the Paris *Western Citizen* in 1826. A local mercantile firm, Hughart and Warfield, inserted a notice featuring "Spears's and William's best Old Whiskey, by the Barrel"; the distillers referred to were Soloman Spears and Samuel Williams.[69] The whiskey made by Spears was so good that it gained what was possibly the best local reputation in the 1820s and 1830s. Daniel Bradford specifically referred to the maker in his auction house notices; "Speare's Old Whiskey"

[66] *Gazette*, March 14, 1839.
[67] *Western Citizen*, May 26, 1843; May 17, 1844.
[68] *Western Citizen*, October 24, 1845.
[69] Ibid., December 2, 1826.

and "40 Bbls. Speare's Prime Old Whiskey" illustrated this recognition.[70] Other distillers who obviously achieved considerable renown were identified in similar fashion. In 1849, the notice of an auction to be held at Millersburg listed "a choice lot of copper distilled Whisky, consisting of about 200 Barrels. Most of said Whisky is of Kellar's make, and 35 or 40 barrels of it is 10 years old."[71] In the following year another Bourbon County sale featured "between 80 and 90 barrels of first rate Bourbon Whisky, 4 years old. It is of John Bedford's manufacture."[72] An announcement in 1850 provided the perfect example of merchandising a distiller's reputation: "Old Bourbon Whisky at Auction. I will sell, on the public square, on the first Monday in December next, 15 barrels of Old Bourbon Whisky, made by Solomon Kellar, one of the best Whisky makers in the world, and this lot not to be surpassed by any."[73]

Also before mid-century, the relatively superior qualities of bourbon whiskey had become a decisive factor in the marketplace. Conclusive evidence is offered by market quotations from the three major port areas of Louisville, Maysville, and Cincinnati. In the first six months of 1848 the aggregate of prices on three descriptions of domestic whiskey—rectified, raw, and unclassified—ranged from a low of fourteen and one quarter cents per gallon to a high of nineteen and one quarter. During the same period, and in the same markets, "Old Bourbon Whiskey" commanded prices which varied from thirty cents to one dollar per gallon, "according to age."[74]

By the time of the Civil War "bourbon" was well on its way to becoming a permanent part of the American language. The experiences of two French visitors to the United States serve to illustrate this point. In the first instance, during General LaFayette's tour of the country (1824–1825), a part of his

[70] *Gazette*, September 12, October 24, November 21, 1835.
[71] *Western Citizen*, November 2, 1849.
[72] Ibid., January 11, 1850.
[73] Ibid., November 15, 1850.
[74] Ibid., January 7, 21, February 25, June 9, 1848.

party's itinerary included a visit to Kentucky and his namesake, Fayette County. Following the visit to "Ashland" a member of the party reported the hospitable offer, tendered by a Kentuckian, of a glass of "wiski" to the health of the guest of honor.[75] Had the finest in Kentucky hospitality been known as bourbon whiskey at the time, it would certainly have been referred to as such. The second of the French visitors, somewhat over a quarter of a century later, was the Prince Napoleon inspecting the camps on Staten Island, in 1861. It was reported that "He tasted a bottle of liquor owned by one of the privates; in fact he not only tasted, but appeared to relish the draught. 'What is it?' said he. 'Old Bourbon Sir,' replied the soldier. 'Old Bourbon indeed,' was the Prince's remark. 'I did not think I would like anything with that name so well.' "[76]

Not only foreigners, but prominent Americans as well, were quite aware of the unique characteristics of the Kentucky product in the decade immediately preceding the Civil War. The versatile Ben Perley Poore visited the Bluegrass state in 1857; in response to a toast, he was quoted as referring to his Kentucky welcome:

Everywhere sir, have I been greeted by gentlemen with "their hearts in their right hands—their right hands in mine," and, must I say it, with bottles of unequalled "Old Bourbon" in their left hands.

> "Long long be my heart with rich memories filled,
> Like a vase in which roses have once been distilled.
> You may break—you may ruin the vase if you will,
> But the scent of that Bourbon will linger there still."[77]

Quite aside from the hyperbole, and after making due allowance for the spirit of the occasion, it is evident from the above sentiment that Kentucky's distilling industry and its principal product had, in slightly over three quarters of a century, come of age.

[75] A. Levasseur, *Lafayette En Amerique, En 1824, et 1825, ou Journal D'Un Voyage aux Etats-Unis* (Paris, 1829), 2:379.
[76] *Western Citizen*, August 30, 1861.
[77] Ibid., September 11, 1857.

7

Bourbon Whiskey:
Miracle & Myth

T HE EXCEEDINGLY VAGUE background of the Kentucky
distilling industry has encouraged the circulation of numerous fanciful and romantic interpretations; this applies equally
to considerations of material, methods, and men. Several of the
more conspicuous misconceptions have already been referred to
in the preceding chapters and these, together with others of a
similarly misleading nature, will be considered in the light of
available documentary evidence.

Not the least of the possible sources of confusion is in connection with the word "bourbon," which was first applied to a newly
created county of eighteenth-century Virginia and subsequently
evolved into the definitive term denoting a whiskey of uniquely
American production. The origin of this word, insofar as it per-
tains to usage in the United States, dates from the Revolutionary
War and the invaluable assistance rendered by the French, whose
ruling house at the time was that of Bourbon. For a number of
years the assignment of French names to the new towns and
counties of the Kentucky area was prompted by what Lewis
Collins termed "the plenitude of good feeling which then existed
toward that nation."[1] Still evident in modern times are conspicuous
examples of this gesture, exemplified by Louisville, Paris, Ver-
sailles, Fayette, and Bourbon. However, the more immediate con-

cern of this investigation relates to the earliest utilization of "bourbon" as descriptive of a type of whiskey and the relationship between Bourbon County and the product which became its namesake.

When Bourbon County was carved out of Fayette (effective in 1786), it formed practically the entire eastern end of the future state of Kentucky. Thirty-four of the present counties, or parts thereof, were at one time included in the single county of Bourbon. This situation remained until the creation of Mason County in 1789, or for a period of three full years. The area's most feasible commercial egress to the Ohio River was through the port of Maysville (Limestone, at first) which had been formally established in 1787.[2] Some indication of the early importance attached to this port may be seen in a Virginia legislative enactment (1784) which ordained the assignment of "two naval officers or collectors" to the Falls of Ohio and the mouth of Limestone.[3]

This port area was of vital significance in the early development of Kentucky. John Filson paid tribute to the settlement in 1785 by noting that "Limestone is the first port of the Kentucke Country."[4] Eight years later the "herborising" Frenchman, André Michaux, observed that "Limestone is considered the landing place or Port of Kentucky."[5] This preeminence continued for a number

[1] Lewis Collins, *Historical Sketches of Kentucky* (Cincinnati, 1847), 192; see also Richard H. Collins, *History of Kentucky* (Covington, 1874), 2:66; George R. Stewart, *Names on the Land* (New York, 1945), 167. The predilection for names of French origin was not limited to Virginia; concurrent with the creation of the Old Dominion's Bourbon County the reigning house of France was likewise honored with the creation of a (short-lived) county in Georgia. See Edmund C. Burnett, comp., "Papers Relating to Bourbon County, Georgia," *American Historical Review* 15 (October 1909):68.

[2] William Waller Hening, comp., *The Statutes at Large: being a Collection of all the Laws of Virginia, from the First Session of the Legislature, in the Year 1619* (Imprint varies, 1819–1823), 12:633.

[3] Ibid., 11:397–98.

[4] Beverly W. Bond, Jr., ed., "Two Westward Journeys of John Filson, 1785," *MVHR* 9 (March 1923):323.

[5] Reuben Gold Thwaites, ed., *Early Western Travels, 1748–1846* (Cleveland, 1904–1907), 3:35.

of years; Maysville was described by Zadok Cramer in 1811 as "the oldest and most accustomed *landing place* on the Ohio."[6] In 1826 the Maysville turnpike committee compiled a report on the yearly commerce of the road between Maysville and Lexington. Based on figures obtained from the "merchants, commission merchants, and dealers" of the port city, there was estimated an annual traffic of 7,636 wagonloads.[7] This total included 2,095 barrels of whiskey which, it might be added, most assuredly did not represent imports.

Since Maysville had quite early become the chief port for a large area of trans-Allegheny Virginia—known for three years as Bourbon County—products originating in the vicinity acquired a designation identifying them with the county. The subsequent reduction of the parent county's size left unchanged the customary association. This fact is particularly evident in the case of whiskey; the identifying name bourbon was used in the vicinity of Maysville and the immediate interior for quite some time before it achieved general usage in the adjoining counties, such as Fayette, or in other port areas, such as Louisville. It appears to have been completely unused in the other whiskey-producing states for a much longer period of time.

The local connotation assigned to "bourbon whiskey" is evident by consideration of an adjacent area; during the period that this designation was becoming popularized for the Kentucky product, similar (perhaps identical) products coming from the distilleries of nearby Tennessee were devoid of such characterization. An advertisement in the Jonesboro *Farmer's Friend* (1825) illustrates the contemporary trend in grain content for distillates: "Wanted immediately, a first rate distiller. A young man without family who understands the art of distilling corn and rye mixed,

[6] Zadok Cramer, *The Navigator* (Pittsburgh, 1811), 106.
[7] Letter of Maysville Turnpike Road Committee to *Maysville Eagle* [1826], Kentucky Historical Society, Frankfort, fol. 653. As late as 1828, Maysville was described as "the next town in Kentucky, in point of commercial importance, to Louisville"; see Timothy Flint, *A Condensed Geography and History of the Western States or the Mississippi Valley* (Cincinnati, 1828), 2:190.

and all rye."[8] Such a mixture of grains could very well have been producing a Tennessee whiskey identical to that of the distillers in the Maysville, Kentucky, trading area. As a matter of fact, other sections of the Bluegrass state were producing whiskey of this same type. This, though not yet categorized as "bourbon whiskey," was produced just as early as that of the area which depended upon Maysville for port facilities. The universality of the corn-rye mixture is evident in an 1831 notice publicizing whiskey specifications for sealed bids at the navy commissioner's office in Washington: "The whiskey must be of the best quality first proof copper distilled, and made of at least one-third rye."[9]

There is considerable evidence that "Old Bourbon" whiskey was the generally accepted nomenclature at first, implying unmistakably that the product originated in the region of "old Bourbon County" rather than expressing a chronological factor in the quality of the goods. Whiskey *from* Old Bourbon was the sole implication in many notices during the 1840s and until well after the middle of the century.[10] A listing of prices current in Maysville represents this trend: "Old Bourbon is worth 37½ @ 1.00 according to age."[11] Occasional advertisements were even more specific: "Old Bourbon Whisky. We have from 100 to 200 Bbls, from 2 to 4 years old for sale."[12] There were great variations in the respective ages of distilled products at this time; all were rather indiscriminately referred to as "Old Bourbon" whiskey. During the decade preceding the Civil War, "Old Bourbon" whis-

[8] Quoted in Paul M. Fink, "The Early Press of Jonesboro," *East Tennessee Historical Society Publications* 10 (1938):62.

[9] *Washington* (D.C.) *Globe*, October 15, 1831. Cited hereafter as *Globe*. This practice came to an end in 1862 with an enactment of the Thirty-Seventh Congress which decreed that "from and after the first day of September, eighteen hundred and sixty-two, the spirit ration in the navy of the United States shall forever cease." U.S., *Statutes at Large*, 12:565. The Army whiskey ration had been discontinued in November 1830. See U.S., Headquarters of the Army, Adjutant General's Office, *Orders, 1829–31*, 34.

[10] *Gazette*, March 14, 1839; March 13, 1841. This is not to say that the benefits of age were completely unrecognized at this time.

[11] *Western Citizen*, January 21, 1848.

[12] Ibid., March 19, 1852.

key was available in quantity at any desired age—ranging from a
low of one year to as high as eleven years.[13] The advertisement of
B. F. Bowen in 1855 is typical of the uncritical use of such terminology: "Old Bourbon Whisky. I have for sale, a lot of No. 1
Bourbon Whisky, 1, 2, 3, and 4 years old, that I will sell on
reasonable terms."[14]

As the reputation of whiskey from "Old Bourbon" gradually
spread, the intent of the nomenclature seems to have been modified
—certainly by the 1840s—to the extent that "Bourbon" (alone)
increasingly became acceptable as descriptive of a regional whiskey. In February of 1849 the wholesale grocery firm of B. F.
Thomas and Company in Maysville offered "130 barrels old and
new Bourbon Whisky."[15] Thomas Eales of Paris notified prospective customers in 1854 that "I have for sale 150 barrels of superior
copper distilled Bourbon whisky, from one to six years old."[16]
Four years later another company of Maysville, R. H. Newell,
featured "1000 Barrels Bourbon Whiskey, 1 to 4 years old."[17] In
this development, Kentuckians were fortunate in that a Kentucky
place-name became synonymous with a widely respected product.
Actually, good whiskey of the same type was, and still is, produced in adjacent states.

It should be noted at this point that the "Bourbon" produced
during this period, for all its merits, could not possibly have met
modern specifications for bourbon whiskey. Currently applicable
federal standards provide that bourbon whiskey be "distilled at not
exceeding 160° proof," and "from a fermented mash of grain of
which not less than 51 percent is corn grain." There is an additional requirement that it be aged in "charred new oak containers" for a minimum of twenty-four calendar months.[18] Herein lies

[13] Ibid., January 3, 1851; May 4, 1855.
[14] Ibid., May 4, 1855.
[15] Ibid., February 23, 1849.
[16] Ibid., November 24, 1854.
[17] *Maysville Express*, March 10, 1858. There clearly continued to be no
discernible effort to make "bourbon" representative of a specific age factor.
[18] U.S., Treasury Department, Internal Revenue Service, Federal Alcoholic Administration, Title 27, *Code of Federal Regulations*, part 5,

the principal difficulty in considering most of the various aspects of early Kentucky distilling—in particular, the first bourbon whiskey. The writers and historians of the late nineteenth century yielded to the temptation of applying their own standards to the distilling practices of the late eighteenth century. Needless to say, these errors have been perpetuated and compounded by the writing profession of a later day.[19]

For the entire period covered by this study (and for several years thereafter) there were no allusions to the one distinguishing visible feature of twentieth-century bourbon whiskey. The required aging process imparts to the whiskey a characteristic reddish-amber color. Without exception, there is no mention of this color factor in travel accounts by the dozen, covering a period of well over a half-century; the same is true of personal reminiscences and records of mercantile operations for a period equally long. Periodic notifications from the Commissary General's Department, soliciting bids for the supply of the whiskey component in Army rations, also fail to mention any age requirement in the desired product, or barrel specification insofar as they related to charred inner surfaces. This is true of the notices covering an entire ten-year period —from the first fully itemized listing which appeared in the Lexington *Gazette* for September 18, 1818, until (and including) the issue for July 20, 1827. In 1820, for example, there was specified "seasoned heart of white oak barrels" for pork, vinegar, whiskey, and flour; in the following year the only barrel requirements were "strong and secure—seasoned heart of oak."[20] Later specifications contained many of the same generalities such as "seasoned heart of

---

"Labeling and Advertising of Distilled Spirits," 27 CFR 5.21, 21524, 21525, 21526, 21528. Compare spelling of "whisky" with that of U.S., *Statutes at Large*, 78:1208 ("whiskey"), as an excellent example of bureaucratic inconsistency.

[19] For examples of reliance on nineteenth-century historians, see Mary Verhoeff, *The Kentucky River Navigation*, Filson Club Publications, no. 28 (Louisville, 1917), 91; Willard Rouse Jillson, *Early Kentucky Distillers, 1783–1800* (Louisville, 1940), xi; Gerald Carson, *The Social History of Bourbon* (New York, 1963), 36, 40.

[20] *Gazette*, August 31, 1820; August 16, 1821.

white oak barrels full hooped," and "at least 16 good hoops."[21] There was never the slightest mention of a charred inner surface for the barrels or allusion to requirements for age of the product. No barrel specifications of any kind appeared in Navy whiskey requirements.

Newspaper advertisements of the period occasionally featured the wares of coopers; their raw material requirements were often included in the same notice. Invariably they specified "seasoned white oak" barrels for sale and used similar terms to describe the desired basic material. However, they consistently failed to mention the one indispensable process for achieving the color of modern bourbon whiskey. Typical notices of cooperage for sale included "a number of tight barrels, Hogsheads, and Double barrels," and "a quantity of Double and Single Barrels . . . well made of good seasoned timber."[22] If any charring of this merchandise took place, it was certainly done by the distiller as a matter of personal preference, not by the cooper as a routine step in the manufacture of whiskey containers.

Several contemporary works on distilling include a considerable amount of detail regarding the stillhouse and its equipment, the methods of distilling, and the ingredients; all are strangely silent on the proper aging of whiskey in a charred oak container and the resulting color. Harrison Hall, in 1818, did go into considerable detail on treating the interior of mash containers for rough spots, splinters, and the like. However, his reasons are more closely related to sanitation than to aging and color. Hall's directions, nevertheless, probably come as near as any known existing account to explaining the origin of the char process for whiskey barrels:

Be very careful to have them well burnt or shaved inside, so that not a blister remain, for if any of these blisters should remain on the inside of the cask, a portion of the contents will insinuate itself under the blister, become acid or putrid, and cause the succeed-

[21] Ibid., July 21, 1826; July 20, 1827.
[22] Ibid., March 22, 1803; December 25, 1806. See also ibid., September 4, 1806; August 18, 1807; August 23, 1808.

ing mash to run rapidly into the acetous or putrefactive, instead of the vinous fermentation; the produce will consequently be decreased, the quality of the spirit vitiated, and the cause will be looked for in vain.[23]

To these instructions Hall added the further admonition that such precautions alone were not enough for the summer months, and it would be necessary to burn the insides with straw. Here is probably the origin of charring whiskey barrels, and it is quite likely that the practice originated in somewhat the manner that Hall outlines—the use of straw or some other flammable material to burn off the rough interior of new oak staves. What began solely as a sterilization process led to an eventual delighted realization that the treatment was contributing materially to the flavor and color of corn whiskey.

A considerable amount of evidence from other sources supports the conclusion that modern standards do not constitute a reliable yardstick for the first half-century of Kentucky distilling. There is no mention in that period of any attempts to limit the use of barrels to the original contents; had charring been practiced at the time, any reuse of these containers would have considerably reduced the effectiveness of the treatment. A great many distillers sold large quantities of their output at retail, popularly known as "by the smalls"; thus there would necessarily have been a large number of barrels used more than once—perhaps on several occasions. In that case any coloring process would have been completely improbable. The same negative result would be applicable in the case of those grocery stores engaged in retailing whiskey, and most of them engaged in the practice. These mercantile establishments were also accustomed to accepting whiskey in payment for their wares—this was an advertised fact and almost without exception. In the hundreds of advertisements consulted, not a single one made any distinction favoring or mentioning whiskey with a color suggestive of the char process.

[23] Harrison Hall, *The Distiller* (Philadelphia, 1818), 94–96.

Other evidence is found in the notifications of the agricultural fairs of the second and third decades of the nineteenth century where there was not the slightest reference to color, either in the entrance requirements or in the competition regulations. They characteristically referred to best sample of "this year's make" or "made in the preceding season." Only flavor and strength were mentioned as criteria of quality. Had there been any process in existence at the time capable of producing a better grade of whiskey or a whiskey distinguished by the characteristic color, this fact would most assuredly have been recognized.

Among connoisseurs of whiskey on the Kentucky scene there was nothing vital about the use of charred barrels; the product resulting from this process simply did not exist in their minds. In 1797 a customer of Governor Shelby's forwarded an order for five double barrels of whiskey; he typically alluded to proof, strength, and taste, but included no mention of color: "I request the favr of you to choose, of the strongest Proof & sweetest taste, If any difference you can find but the whole seemed so equal in taste, as well as strength, that you must be somewhat at a loss to make a choice, you'll please to mark them with the red chalk which follows."[24] Had a whiskey answering to the specifications of today's bourbon been available, those establishments catering to discriminating drinkers would have been the first to recognize and capitalize on the possibilities. Several of Kentucky's prominent houses of refreshment—the Exchange Coffee House (Paris), the Phoenix Hotel (Lexington), the La Fayette Coffee House (Lexington), and the Tontine House (Lexington)—periodically featured such beverages as St. Croix Rum, Holland Gin, Old Cogniac Brandy, Old Peach Brandy, ten-year old Irish Whiskey, and exotic assortments of wines and cordials. However, there was no mention of any product that answered the specifications for bourbon whiskey of a latter day.[25]

[24] Hare to Shelby, October 6, 1797, Shelby Family Papers, Library of Congress.
[25] *Western Citizen*, December 25, 1830; *Gazette*, January 18, October 18, 1834; July 21, 1836.

Historical honesty requires some reference to a horrid practice. On occasion, the works of distilling authorities contained detailed instructions for making artificial liquors of various kinds, including bourbon. A recipe of 1858 lists the additives for making imitation bourbon whiskey from rectified corn whiskey, including one pound of the essence of Bourbon, one ounce of sweet spirits of nitre, one gallon of syrup, and four barrels of common rectified corn whiskey.[26] The conversion of rectified whiskey into artificial bourbon whiskey had by then become popularized on the state level; a western Kentucky newspaper in 1856 carried notice of a "patent process" for changing rectified whiskey into Monongahela Rye, Old Virginia Malt, or Bourbon.[27] Admittedly, this was an indication of the widespread acceptance of bourbon whiskey, but nothing in these recipes would indicate that the achievement of a reddish color was one of the desired results. All of which leads to an inescapable conclusion: there were no color requirements for bourbon whiskey during perhaps the entire first half of the nineteenth century, and during the same period there was no widespread practice of charring the oak barrels in which the whiskey was aged. Kentucky whiskey had undoubtedly begun to achieve considerable recognition during the latter years of this period, but it is entirely misleading to apply unqualified modern connotations in referring to the product.[28]

Of considerable influence in contributing to a misconception of early bourbon were the personal reminiscences of a few Kentuckians who, writing in the latter part of the nineteenth century, had a tendency to color their accounts of the past with the terminology of a later day. Two excellent examples of this inclination occur in the writings of Cassius Clay and Ebenezer Hiram Stedman.

[26] Lewis Feuchtwanger, *Fermented Liquors: A Treatise on Brewing, Distilling, Rectifying, and Manufacturing of Sugars, Wines, Spirits . . .* (New York, 1858), 88.

[27] *Hickman Times*, July 2, 1856.

[28] The *Lexington Gazette* reported that Santa Anna, the Mexican general and politician, made free use of American whiskey while he was a prisoner in Texas; however, he was credited with calling it "vino de Kentuck" at that time. *Gazette*, September 21, 1844.

Clay, writing in the mid-1880s and describing events of his boyhood some sixty to sixty-five years before, depicted the early morning practice of his father—partaking of "some native bourbon" in a prebreakfast ritual—in the accustomed words of the late nineteenth century rather than those more accurately descriptive of actual conditions.

This same tendency marks the reminiscences of Ebenezer Hiram Stedman, the Scott County paper manufacturer, who also wrote of conditions in the 1820s and 1830s from the vantage point of the mid-1880s. Stedman's work, characterized by numerous references to bourbon whiskey, provides a colorful description of Scott County mores in the earlier days: ". . . & when we got to Combs tavern near the Cathlick Church we all got a drink of Good old Burbon Sperits."[29] In writing of practices followed by the "Izaak Waltons" of that day Stedman related: "They Brot the Best provisions and alwais The Best of old Burbon not to drink to Excess, But to Make one Feel Renewed after the toils of Fishing"; on the occasion of a deer hunt, he remembered, "We ware in fine Sperits; had plenty of that old Burbon along."[30]

The historian of Bourbon County (and others), William Henry Perrin, showed a like inclination to refer to "bourbon whiskey" as though it were being so categorized as early as 1789, while writing under the influence of his 1882 environment. Perrin was undoubtedly influenced by the work of Richard Collins in the preceding decade; there is marked similarity in the words of both when referring to the "bourbon whiskey" of pre-1800 Kentucky.

Of all the unsubstantiated theories regarding the distilling industry, without doubt the most interesting pertain to individual involvement—for example, "the distiller of the first bourbon whiskey," or the equally intriguing "first distiller of Kentucky." In either case it is the unsupported version of a nineteenth-century historian which appears to be the sole basis for subsequent un-

[29] Frances L. S. Dugan and Jacqueline P. Bull, eds., *Bluegrass Craftsman: Being the Reminiscences of Ebenezer Hiram Stedman, Papermaker, 1808–1885* (Lexington, 1959), 149.
[30] Ibid., 181, 185.

qualified acceptance as fact. Richard Collins apparently started the Baptist minister, the Reverend Elijah Craig, on the road to fame with his pronouncement that "the first Bourbon Whiskey was made in 1789, at Georgetown, at the fulling mill at the Royal spring."[31] This statement was first published in 1874, completely devoid of supplemental verification, and has since been accepted by historians and writers at face value. Local historians in the wake of Collins have faithfully repeated this allegation with no apparent attempt to examine or confirm it.[32] Understandably, modern journalists and writers concerned with industrial publicity have been happy to accept this charming legend.[33]

However, with respect to the kind of bourbon whiskey that we recognize as such today, Craig's product is no more deserving of the honor, than that of the nameless hundreds of other distillers of his time. Elijah was making exactly the same kind of whiskey that most of his contemporaries were making; depending on the availability of grain at the time, they were producing either pure corn whiskey or corn whiskey with a small amount of rye in it. The writer knows of no valid evidence which would indicate that Craig (or anyone else at the time) was deliberately charring his barrels to achieve the full benefits of both age and color in the storage of his whiskey.

Furthermore, Elijah Craig's distillery was never located in Bourbon County, as several writers of a later date have described it.[34] During the time when the good divine was allegedly making "the first bourbon" at the Royal Spring, he would have been in

[31] Collins, *History of Kentucky*, 1:516.

[32] William Henry Perrin, *History of Bourbon, Scott, Harrison, and Nicholas Counties, Kentucky* (Chicago, 1882), 156; Verhoeff, *Kentucky River Navigation*, 95.

[33] "An early if not the first commercial distillery in Kentucky was set up at Georgetown by a Baptist minister in 1789." Howard T. Walden, *Native Inheritance: the Story of Corn in America* (New York, 1966), 131. See also H. F. Willkie, *Beverage Spirits in America* (New York, 1949), 18; Harold J. Grossman, *Grossman's Guide to Wines, Spirits, and Beers* (New York, 1964), 249.

[34] Willkie, *Beverage Spirits in America*, 20; Grossman, *Guide to Wines*, 249.

either Fayette or Woodford County; the Georgetown area was a part of Fayette County from November 1, 1780, until May 1, 1789, when it was included in the newly formed Woodford County. On September 1, 1792, Scott County was established. Thus, technically speaking, six years after moving to Kentucky the Reverend Mr. Craig found himself a resident of Scott County.

Perhaps the most conclusive evidence of all with regard to Elijah and his *not* making the first bourbon whiskey (certainly not known as bourbon at the time) lies in the oratory of a Jackson dinner in Frankfort on September 10, 1827, when Lewis Sanders offered the following volunteer toast:

The memory of Elijah Craig, the founder of Georgetown, Kentucky. A philosopher and Christian—an useful man in his day. He established the first fulling mill, the first paper mill and the first rope walk in Kentucky. Honor to whom honor is done.[35]

Since Sanders, in 1810, had owned one of the largest distilling operations of the day, he should certainly have been familiar with "the first bourbon whiskey" by Craig—if there was anything to the story. Furthermore, one of Elijah's close associates, Judge Harry Innes (his lawyer), never alluded to this matter in his private papers.[36] Craig was certainly engaged in making whiskey in the period immediately following the enactment of the first excise; his tax troubles of the 1790s indicate this. As a matter of fact, Scott County led all of the Kentucky counties in the number of tax infractions prosecuted by the federal government. It is possible that Craig and his fellow distillers were producing a copper-distilled, double-distilled, sour-mash type of whiskey, and the finished proof may possibly have met modern specifications. It is most unlikely, however, that this whiskey was bourbon as we know it today.

The indolent human tendency to accept and perpetuate errors, once they are committed to print, was never better illustrated than in the practice of crediting Evan Williams of Louisville with being

[35] *Argus*, September 19, 1827.
[36] Innes Papers.

the first distiller of Kentucky. This mistaken idea originated with
Colonel Reuben Durrett in 1892, when he mentioned that "as
early as 1783, whisky had been distilled from corn." This information was supported by the following implicational footnote:

In 1783, Evan Williams erected a small distillery on the river
at the foot of Fifth street, in Louisville. Here he distilled whisky
from corn, and the dwellers among the ponds at the falls thought
his product a good medicine for chills and fever, though a very
bad whisky. Williams, as a manufacturer of whisky, claimed the
right to sell his product without license, but in March, 1788, he
was indicted by the grand jury for this offense. In 1802, the water
and slop from his distillery became so offensive to those dwelling
near that his establishment was declared a nuisance. Williams was
a member of the early board of trustees of Louisville, and *tradition
says* that he never attended a meeting of the board without bringing a bottle of his whisky, and that what he brought was always
drank [*sic*] by the members before the meeting adjourned.[37]

Williams was, indeed, an early distiller; however if he didn't
get started before 1783, he could hardly be credited with being the
first in Kentucky. He may possibly have been first in the immediate
environs of Louisville, even though this is subject to some question.
At any rate, the historians and writers of a later day have un-
critically repeated this information, thereby ignoring the eight
years of pre-1783 settlement during which distilling was practiced by a large percentage of the settlers.

During this period the frontiersmen who owned stills customarily furnished them for the use of their less fortunate neighbors. Because of the largely unrecorded nature of pioneer life and
the usual absence of production records, it would be impossible to
designate *unequivocally* a "first distiller of Kentucky." Some of the
best claims to the honor, accompanied by a certain amount of
documentation, would be those of a few practitioners in the area of
(at that time) Lincoln County. Jacob Myers, in particular, is a

[37] Reuben Thomas Durrett, *The Centenary of Kentucky*, Filson Club
Publications, no. 7 (Louisville, 1892), 79.

likely candidate for the distinction. The major basis for this allegation is the pension statement of Captain Henry Wilson, a one-time
member of Harrod's regiment, a survivor of the Battle of Blue
Licks, and a veteran of General Clark's first campaign.[38] At the
time Wilson supplied this information he was seventy-two years of
age and living in Bourbon County; he had migrated to Kentucky in
the fall of 1779. Wilson's deposition included information on
three of the early distillers of Kentucky (c. 1780–1781):

Squire Boone was in 1780, elected burgess for Lincoln; and in
[Apr ?] 81, the Lincoln District sent Ben Logan—against old
Jacob Myers, who had a distillery on Dick's river, the first proba-
bly in Ky.—save a couple of small copper 40 gallon stills brought
over on pack horses, the one by Joseph Davis [sic] at the Low
Dutch Station, near Harrod's Station—his brother Samuel at
Whitley's Station. Myers made free use of his whiskey, but the
old Indian fighter distanced him and was easily elected.[39]

In the case of Jacob Myers, these facts agree with those of
Benjamin Logan's biographer regarding the 1781 election of
burgesses.[40] Myers also petitioned the Lincoln County court, in
June 1783, for permission to erect a mill on the south side of
Dick's River near its junction with the Hanging Fork. As previously noted, it was then customary for distilleries and grist mills
to be located and operated conjointly. Myers's mill was undoubtedly in use before the November term of court in 1783; at
that time it was being used as a place name for a local road.[41]

According to Lewis Collins, in 1779 Samuel Daviess moved
from Bedford County, Virginia, to Whitley's Station in Lincoln
County; his brother James lived five miles distant.[42] At the April
term of the Lincoln County court Samuel Davis [sic] was ap-

[38] Lyman C. Draper Manuscripts, State Historical Society of Wisconsin,
9 J 34, 9 J 37; Collins, *History of Kentucky*, 1:6; 2:183, 663.
[39] Ibid., 9 J 34.
[40] Charles Gano Talbert, *Benjamin Logan: Kentucky Frontiersman*
(Lexington, 1962), 127.
[41] Lincoln County Order Book 1, 104, 138; see also note 44 below.
[42] Collins, *Historical Sketches*, 403–05.

pointed deputy surveyor.[43] John Filson's "Map of Kentucke" locates Whitley's Station approximately fourteen and one quarter miles from the Low Dutch Station in a southeasterly direction; the map (1784) also includes "Myres" mill.[44]

Henry Wilson's information relative to the Daviess brothers included a graphic description of frontier practices on the occasion of sickness and death:

The Daviess—Joe and Sam both Irish[.] Jo lived the Low Dutch Station near Harrod's Station, in Mercer County, and his brother Sam at Whitley's in Lincoln. They used to brag over each other as to wh. made the best whiskey. Jo was the father of late Col Jo H. Daviess. Samuel was taken sick and expected not to live and sent for his brother, Joe ordered his Jinny to get his clothes and a bottle of his best, and off he went. He found his brother Sam dead—Sam, too, had a Jenny, and she, poor soul, almost broken hearted, was weeping bitterly, over the dead body of her lamented —with a house full of consoling neighbors around her. "Well," said Jo mournfully, "Sam is dead"—"Yes" replied the poor widow, "he is gone," and sobbed as if her heart would break. "Tut Jenny, wipe up your eyes, he's only a dead man now, and not worth crying about; you made him a good wife while he was with you —all you can do, Jenny, is to bury him decently. Come, wipe up your eyes; here" continued Joe drawing out his bottle from his hunting shirt pocket—"here Jenney, come take a bear of this, its good old Mercer whiskey, none of your Lincoln stinkabust, such as Sam used to make." Note—this occurred after the division of Lincoln and formation of Mercer County.[45]

Another early Kentuckian with a shadowy claim to being one of the first distillers was William Calk, who migrated to Kentucky in 1775 from Prince William County in Virginia. Calk is known to have come from a distillery-owning family of some means. Ap-

---

[43] Collins, *History of Kentucky*, 2:476.

[44] Copy of this map in possession of the author.

[45] Draper Manuscripts, 9 J 37. Additional information on Colonel Joseph Hamilton Daveiss [*sic*] and his parents, Joseph and Jean, may be found in *The Biographical Encyclopaedia of Kentucky of the Dead and Living Men of the Nineteenth Century* (Cincinnati, 1878), 526–27.

parently he left no detailed records of his activities in Kentucky after settling in what is now Montgomery County; this applies particularly to the prosaic occupation of distilling grain mash. However, fragmentary records do show that he was trying to buy some stills in 1786, and he may possibly have possessed one prior to that date. There is little doubt that Calk was successful in obtaining his distilling equipment; during the following three years he engaged in selling whiskey in quantities as large as five gallons per customer.[46] Calk's location was a part of Bourbon County from 1786 to 1793; it did not become Montgomery County until March 1, 1797.

Appropriately enough, the first governor of Kentucky has unassailable claim to being a prominent early distiller. Like Calk, Isaac Shelby came from a distilling family; after his migration to Kentucky, Shelby entered the distilling business in his own right. His troubles with the Internal Revenue collectors have already been recounted. Governor Shelby is known to have been a very busy distiller during the final decade of the eighteenth century and the opening years of the nineteenth, and it is quite likely that he was active in the business much earlier than this, possibly as early as the mid-1780s. Shelby's production of whiskey was, for its day, quite large; in 1797 the governor promised one good customer, "I will deliver to Mr Andrew O Hare seven hundred and three gallons of good whiskey in eleven casks at my house when therto required & which he has this day bought of me."[47]

It would be possible to list dozens of early Kentucky citizens—prominent and otherwise—with some claim to fame in this category. In every instance, however, there are significant omissions regarding the details of their distilling activities, and for this there are good reasons. In the life of the pioneer, distilling was no more a noteworthy avocation than was the routine hog-killing following the advent of cold weather. More importantly to the annals of

---

[46] William Calk, Papers, 1783–1799. Photocopies in University of Kentucky Library, Lexington.

[47] Receipt by Isaac Shelby, July 28, 1797, Shelby Family Papers.

whiskey, the early historians of Kentucky failed to provide any-thing resembling adequate coverage of the initial phases of the distilling industry—this is without exception. The works of Humphrey Marshall (1812), Mann Butler (1834), and Lewis Collins (1847) are indisputably valuable contributions to the early political history of Kentucky; this cannot be said of their coverage of the state's most important early commercial under-taking.

Marshall's only mention of whiskey is typical—he allocates a grand total of perhaps one page to the effects of the Pennsylvania Whiskey Rebellion and the enforcement of the excise tax in Ken-tucky. As has been noted, Marshall was completely out of sympathy with the problems of the small distiller, with the efforts to obtain redress of grievance, and particularly with the subsequent attempts at tax evasion. Butler's coverage of whiskey production was equally unsatisfactory, though he does mention that "some dis-tilleries were erected for the distillation of spirits from Indian corn" on the south side of the Kentucky River.[48] As Butler was referring to the year 1783, this is probably the source of the "1783 myth" so effectively perpetuated by Richard Collins and others.

Lewis Collins supplied only the barest minimum of words re-lating to the distilling industry; his son's enlarged revision (1874) of the earlier Collins work adds a few unsubstantiated facts, some obviously from Butler, but includes no real treatment of the sub-ject. The most likely reason for Lewis Collins's almost total neglect of the subject was his involvement in the incipient temperance movement. At the time that he was writing his history, Collins was an officer in the Limestone Division of the Sons of Temperance.[49]

The widely quoted local historians, both of county and town, were just as misleading in their treatment of a poorly researched subject, and even worse in their obvious display of temperance-influenced bias. This grouping would include annalists such as

[48] Mann Butler, *A History of the Commonwealth of Kentucky* (Louis-ville, 1834), 142; Collins, *History of Kentucky*, 1:20.
[49] *Western Citizen*, October 1, 1847.

M'Murtrie (1819), Casseday (1852), and Perrin (1882), to name only a few. As one of the earliest writers on Louisville, M'Murtrie provided excellent coverage of the Hope Distillery in his *Sketches of Louisville and Its Environs;* he then proceeded to expatiate at great length on the evils of whiskey. With M'Murtrie, whiskey became "this demoralizing beverage"; his objectivity broke down completely as he continued: "my feeble voice can be but of little utility, in preventing the erection of such gigantic reservoirs of this damning drink! . . . [those instrumental] are mere manufacturers of *poison* for the human race."[50] Thomas M. Gilmore, in Johnston's *Memorial History of Louisville*, faithfully repeats most of the Hope Distillery information from this "learned author" (M'Murtrie), but does charitably omit the banalities.[51] Casseday's treatment of the Hope Distillery is similar to that of M'Murtrie: "As if to counterbalance the prospective evil likely to be produced by this enormous manufactory of 'poison for soul and body,' there was established about the same time the first Presbyterian Church in Louisville."[52]

William Henry Perrin, the previously mentioned historian of several Kentucky counties (Fayette, Bourbon, Scott, Harrison, and Nicholas), followed in the best tradition of the temperance-influenced school of Kentucky historians. Discussing the distilling industry in Bourbon County, Perrin expressed cold righteousness: "That whisky is a valuable commercial interest in this part of the State, and that the revenue derived from its sale and manufacture is large, is a fact beyond dispute; that it is a foe, bitter and relentless to Christian civilization, is a fact equally palpable."[53] With equal sympathy, Perrin examined the whiskey situation in Nicholas County. Admitting its early start, he continues: "But, in later

[50] H. M'Murtrie, *Sketches of Louisville and Its Environs* (Louisville, 1819), 130–31.

[51] J. Stoddard Johnston, ed., *Memorial History of Louisville from Its First Settlement to the Year 1896* (Chicago, 1896), 1:263.

[52] Ben Casseday, *The History of Louisville from Its Earliest Settlement Till the Year 1852* (Louisville, 1852), 143.

[53] Perrin, *History of Bourbon, Scott, Harrison and Nicholas Counties*, 65.

years, the people have advanced a step above this rather question-able business, devoting their talents and energies to more credit-able, if less remunerative, callings."[54] For Scott County, Perrin reserved this blast: "The blue grass region has kept up its reputa-tion for good whisky, and still makes the best in the world—if the word *good* may be, without violence, applied to the greatest known evil in existence."[55]

From such intolerant writers, a thorough and objective treatment of the distilling industry was not to be expected. There was never a serious attempt on the part of the nineteenth-century historians of Kentucky to perform the necessary research. Thus was much valuable history lost, perhaps beyond recall, and therefore arose many pleasant legends in its stead.

[54] Ibid., 341.
[55] Ibid., 164.

Bibliography

I. Manuscripts

Bodley, Major Thomas. MS Receipt (fol. 88). Kentucky Historical Society, Frankfort.

Bryan's Station Church. Minute Book, 1786–1895 (typescript). University of Kentucky Library, Lexington.

Calk, William. MS Journal, 1775 (photocopy). University of Kentucky Library, Lexington.

———. Papers, 1783–1799. Photocopies in University of Kentucky Library, Lexington.

Clark, John B. MS Papers (fol. 173-A). Kentucky Historical Society, Frankfort.

Clark, William. Account Book, 1812–1861. Filson Club, Louisville.

Distillery Day Book, March 6, 1833, to June 21, 1833. Blue Lick Museum, Blue Lick Springs, Kentucky.

Draper, Lyman C. Manuscripts. Originals at State Historical Society of Wisconsin, Madison; microfilm copies in University of Kentucky Library, Lexington.

Howell, Ezekial. MS letter to Thomas Bodley, August 25, 1797 (fol. 460). Kentucky Historical Society, Frankfort.

Innes, Harry. MS letter to John Brown, December 7, 1787 (fol. 473). Kentucky Historical Society, Frankfort.

———. Papers, 1772–1850. Library of Congress.

Jamieson, Neil. Papers, 1757–1789. Library of Congress.

M'Donald, James, and Thruston, Charles M. Account Books, 1794–1797. Filson Club, Louisville.

Marble Creek Baptist Church. Minute Book, 1787–1842 (typescript). University of Kentucky Library, Lexington.

Maysville Turnpike Road Committee. MS letter to Maysville *Eagle* [1826] (fol. 653). Kentucky Historical Society, Frankfort.

Perry, Fountain, and Perry, Roderick. Papers, 1800–1839. University of Kentucky Library, Lexington.

Shelby, Evan. MS agreement with Peirce Wall, February 19, 1780 (fol. 850). Kentucky Historical Society, Frankfort.

Shelby Family. Papers. Originals in Library of Congress; microfilm copies in University of Kentucky Library, Lexington.

South Elkhorn Christian Church. Minute Book, 1817–1897. Lexington Theological Seminary.

Taylor, Jonathan. Manuscript Diary, 1774–1815 (?). Filson Club, Louisville.

Wallace, Arthur A. Papers, 1834–1835. Filson Club, Louisville.

Washington, Kentucky. Account Book, 1795–1797. Blue Lick Museum, Blue Lick Springs, Kentucky.

Wilson, Rudolph. Distillery Day Book, 1855–1864. Blue Lick Museum, Blue Lick Springs, Kentucky.

II. Documents and Works of a Public Nature

Acts Passed at the First Session of the Seventh General Assembly, for the Commonwealth of Kentucky. Frankfort: Hunter and Beaumont, 1799.

Biographical Directory of the American Congress, 1774–1949. Washington, D.C.: Government Printing Office, 1950.

Brownson, Charles B., comp. *Congressional Staff Directory, 1964.* Washington, D.C., 1964.

Coxe, Tench. *A Statement of the Arts and Manufactures of the United States of America, for the Year 1810.* Philadelphia: A. Cornman, Jr., 1814.

Hening, William Waller, comp. *The Statutes at Large: being a Collection of all the Laws of Virginia, from the First Session of the Legislature, in the Year 1619.* 13 vols. Imprint varies, 1819–1823.

Hunter, Alfred, comp. *A Catalogue Showing the Location of Every Model of Patented Inventions, in the New Hall of the Patent Office, with the Class to Which it belongs; . . .* Washington, D.C.: J. Kirkwood, 1855.

Irdell, James, comp. *Laws of the State of North Carolina.* Edenton, N.C.: Hodge and Wills, 1791.

Kentucky. Circuit and county court records.

Littell, William, comp. *The Statute Law of Kentucky.* . . . 5 vols. Frankfort: William Hunter and Others, 1809–1819.

——, and Swigert, Jacob, comps. *A Digest of the Statute Law of Kentucky.* 2 vols. Frankfort: Kendall and Russell, 1822.

Miller, Hunter, comp. *Treaties and Other International Acts of the United States of America.* 8 vols. Washington, D.C.: Government Printing Office, 1931–1948.

Morehead, C. S., and Brown, Mason, comps. *A Digest of the Statute Laws of Kentucky.* . . . 2 vols. Frankfort: Albert G. Hodges, 1834.

Pirtle, Henry, comp. *A Digest of the Decisions of the Court of Appeals of Kentucky.* 2 vols. Louisville: S. Penn, Jr., 1832.

Thorpe, Francis Newton, comp. *The Federal and State Constitutions, Colonial Charters, and Other Organic Laws of the States, Territories, and Colonies now or Heretofore Forming the United States of America.* 7 vols. Washington, D.C.: Government Printing Office, 1909.

Toulmin, Harry, comp. *A Collection of All the Public and Permanent Acts of the General Assembly of Kentucky.* . . . Frankfort: William Hunter, 1802.

U.S., Congress, *American State Papers.* 38 vols. *Military Affairs,* 4, 5; *Finance,* 1, 3; *Miscellaneous,* 1, 2. Washington, D.C.: Gales and Seaton, 1832–1861.

——. *Congressional Record.* Vol. 110, 1964.

——. *Debates and Proceedings in the Congress of the United States, 1789–1824.* 42 vols. (Vols. 2–6.) Washington, D.C.: Gales and Seaton, 1834–1856.

——. House Executive Documents. 22d Cong., 1st sess., December 7, 1831; 22d Cong., 2d sess., December 3, 1832. Washington, D.C.: Duff Green, 1831, 1832.

——. *Journals of the American Congress, 1774–1788.* 4 vols. Washington, D.C.: Way and Gideon, 1823.

——. *Register of Debates in Congress, 1825–1837.* 29 vols. (Vols. 7–9.) Washington, D.C.: Gales and Seaton, 1825–1837.

U.S., District Court Records. (Kentucky District, Harrodsburg, 1783–1786; Kentucky District, Harrodsburg and Frankfort, 1789–1800; Kentucky, Eastern District, 1795–1801).

U.S., Headquarters of the Army, Adjutant General's Office. *Orders, 1829–31; Orders, 1832–33.*

U.S., *Statutes at Large.* Vols. 1–3, 5, 7, 12, 13, 69, 78.

U.S., Treasury Department, Bureau of Internal Revenue. *Gauging Manual*. Washington, D.C.: Government Printing Office, 1950.

U.S., Treasury Department, Internal Revenue Service, Alcohol and Tobacco Tax Division. "History and Development of the Taxing Laws." Internal Revenue Service Publication no. 17468 (mimeographed, n.d.).

————. "Laws Imposing Tax with Respect to Distilled Spirits." Internal Revenue Service Publication no. 17470 (mimeographed, n.d.).

U.S., Treasury Department, Internal Revenue Service, Federal Alcohol Administration. Title 27, *Code of Federal Regulations*, part 5, "Labeling and Advertising of Distilled Spirits," as amended, 1960.

Virginia. Circuit and county court records.

III. Newspapers and Periodicals

A. NEWSPAPERS*

Bardstown Herald. (1831–1836)
Bardstown Western Herald. (1825–1828)
Cincinnati [Ohio] *Centinel of the North-Western Territory.* (1793–1796)
Cincinnati [Ohio] *Inquisitor and Cincinnati Advertiser.* (1818–1822)
Danville Olive Branch. (1820–1826)
Frankfort Argus of Western America. (1808–1838)
Frankfort Commentator. (1828–1830)
Georgetown Patriot. (1816)
Georgetown Telegraph. (1812)
Harrodsburg Ploughboy. (1849)
Hickman Times. (1856)
Hickman Weekly Commercial Standard. (1845)
Lexington Kentucky Gazette. (1787–1848)
Lexington Kentucky Reporter. (1829)
Lexington Observer and Kentucky Reporter. (1833)
Lexington Western Monitor. (1814–1816)
Louisville Correspondent. (1814–1817)

* From Kentucky towns unless otherwise indicated.

Louisville Courier-Journal. (1967)

Louisville Daily Journal. (1830–1831)

Maysville Express. (1858)

Mount Sterling Columbian Spy. (1824–1825)

Paris Western Citizen. (1808–1861)

Pennsylvania Evening Herald [Philadelphia]. (1785–1788)

Russellville Farmer's Friend. (1809–1810)

Russellville Mirror. (1806–1807)

Stewart's Kentucky Herald [Lexington]. (1795–1801)

Washington [D.C.] *Globe.* (1830–1831)

Williamsburg [Va.] *Virginia Gazette.* (1736–1739)

B. PERIODICALS

Cramer's Pittsburgh Almanac. Vol. 5, 1808; vol. 12, 1813.

Hunt's Merchants' Magazine and Commercial Review [New York]. Vols. 1–4, 1839–1841.

IV. Collected Documents

Acrelius, Israel. *A History of New Sweden: or, The Settlements on the River Delaware.* Translated by William M. Reynolds. Philadelphia: Historical Society of Pennsylvania, 1876.

Adams, Charles Francis, Jr., ed. *The New England Canaan of Thomas Morton.* Boston: Prince Society, 1883.

Adams, Henry, ed. *The Writing of Albert Gallatin.* 3 vols. Philadelphia: J. B. Lippincott and Co., 1879.

Arber, Edward, ed. *Travels and Works of Captain John Smith, President of Virginia, and Admiral of New England, 1580–1631.* 2 vols. Edinburgh: John Grant, 1910.

Baldwin, Leland D. "Orders Issued by General Henry Lee During the Campaign against the Whiskey Insurrectionists." *Western Pennsylvania Historical Magazine* 19 (June 1936): 79–111.

Boyd, William K., ed. *Some Eighteenth Century Tracts Concerning North Carolina.* Raleigh: Edwards and Broughton Company, 1927.

Carman, Harry J., ed. *American Husbandry.* Columbia University Studies in the History of American Agriculture, no. 6. New York: Columbia University Press, 1939.

Clift, G. Glenn, comp. *"Second Census" of Kentucky, 1800.* Frankfort: privately published, 1954.

Davis, William T., ed. *Bradford's History of Plymouth Plantation, 1606–1646.* In *Original Narratives of Early American History.* Edited by J. Franklin Jameson. New York: Charles Scribner's Sons, 1908.

Fitzpatrick, John C., ed. *The Writings of George Washington from the Original Manuscript Sources, 1745–1799.* 37 vols. Washington, D.C.: Government Printing Office, 1931–1941.

Fries, Adelaide L., ed. *Records of the Moravians in North Carolina, 1752–1822.* 8 vols. Raleigh: North Carolina Historical Commission, 1922–1954.

Grimes, J. Bryan, comp. *North Carolina Wills and Inventories.* Raleigh: Edwards and Broughton, 1912.

Heinemann, Charles B., comp. *First Census of Kentucky, 1790.* Baltimore: Southern Book Co., 1956.

Hunt, Gaillard, ed. *The Writings of James Madison.* 9 vols. New York: G. P. Putnam's Sons, 1900–1910.

James, James Alton, ed. *George Rogers Clark Papers, 1771–1781,* and *1781–1784.* Collections of the Illinois State Historical Library, vol. 8, Virginia Series, vol. 3, and vol. 19, Virginia Series, vol. 4. Springfield: Illinois State Historical Library, 1912, 1926.

Jillson, Willard Rouse, ed. "Index of Minute Book A (1780–1783), Jefferson County Court, Virginia." *Register of the Kentucky Historical Society* 53 (January 1955): 37–57.

Lefler, Hugh Talmage, ed. *North Carolina History Told by Contemporaries.* Chapel Hill: University of North Carolina Press, 1948.

Lodge, Henry Cabot, ed. *The Works of Alexander Hamilton.* 12 vols. New York: G. P. Putnam's Sons, 1904.

Myers, Albert Cook, ed. *Narratives of Early Pennsylvania, West New Jersey, and Delaware, 1630–1707.* In *Original Narratives of Early American History.* Edited by J. Franklin Jameson. New York: Charles Scribner's Sons, 1912.

Paltsits, Victor Hugo, ed. *Minutes of the Executive Council of the Province of New York, 1668–1673.* 2 vols. Albany: State of New York, 1910.

Prucha, Francis Paul, ed. *Army Life on the Western Frontier: Selections from the Official Reports Made between 1826 and 1845 by Colonel George Croghan.* Norman: University of Oklahoma Press, 1958.

Robertson, James Rood, ed. *Petitions of the Early Inhabitants of*

Kentucky to the General Assembly of Virginia, 1769–1792. Filson Club Publications, no. 27. Louisville: John P. Morton and Co., 1914.

Salley, Alexander S., Jr., ed. *Narratives of Early Carolina, 1650–1708.* In *Original Narratives of Early American History.* Edited by J. Franklin Jameson. New York: Charles Scribner's Sons, 1911.

Summers, Lewis Preston, comp. *Annals of Southwest Virginia, 1769–1800.* Abingdon, Va.: L. P. Summers, 1929.

Syrett, Harold C., ed. *The Papers of Alexander Hamilton.* In progress. New York: Columbia University Press, 1961– .

Thwaites, Reuben Gold, ed. *Early Western Travels, 1748–1846.* 32 vols. Cleveland: Arthur H. Clark Co., 1904–1907.

Tyler, Lyon Gardiner, ed. *Narratives of Early Virginia, 1606–1625.* In *Original Narratives of Early American History.* Edited by J. Franklin Jameson. New York: Charles Scribner's Sons, 1907.

V. Diaries, Journals, and Memoirs

"Autobiographical Sketch of the Life of Gen. John Burrows, of Lycoming Co., Penna." *Pennsylvania Magazine of History and Biography* 34 (1910): 419–37.

Baldwin, Thomas. *Narrative of the Massacre, by the Savages of the Wife and Children of Thomas Baldwin. . . .* New York: Martin and Perry, 1836.

Bond, Beverley W., Jr., ed. "Two Westward Journeys of John Filson, 1785." *Mississippi Valley Historical Review* 9 (March 1923): 320–30.

Cartwright, Peter. *The Backwoods Preacher: An Autobiography.* London: A. Heylin, 1858.

Clay, Cassius Marcellus. *The Life of Cassius Marcellus Clay: Memoirs, Writings and Speeches.* Cincinnati: J. Fletcher Brennan and Co., 1886.

Cresswell, Nicholas. *The Journal of Nicholas Cresswell, 1774–1777.* London: Jonathan Cape, 1925.

Drake, Daniel. *Pioneer Life in Kentucky, 1785–1800.* Edited by Emmet Field Horine. New York: Henry Schuman, 1948.

Dugan, Frances L. S., and Bull, Jacqueline P., eds. *Bluegrass Craftsman: Being the Reminiscences of Ebenezer Hiram Sted-*

man, *Papermaker, 1808–1885.* Lexington: University of Kentucky Press, 1959.

Farish, Hunter Dickenson, ed. *Journal and Letters of Philip Vickers Fithian, 1773–1774: A Plantation Tutor of the Old Dominion.* Williamsburg: Colonial Williamsburg, Inc., 1943.

Fitzpatrick, John C., ed. *The Diaries of George Washington, 1748–1799.* 4 vols. Boston: Houghton Mifflin Co., 1925.

Greene, Jack P., ed. *The Diary of Colonel Landon Carter of Sabine Hall, 1752–1778.* 2 vols. Charlottesville: University of Virginia Press, 1965.

Harrison, Lowell H. "A Virginian Moves to Kentucky, 1793." *William and Mary Quarterly* 3d ser., 15 (April 1958): 201–13.

Jillson, Willard Rouse, ed. *Tales of the Dark and Bloody Ground: A Group of Fifteen Original Papers on the Early History of Kentucky.* Louisville: C. T. Dearing Printing Co., 1930.

Kilpatrick, Lewis H., ed. "The Journal of William Calk, Kentucky Pioneer." *Mississippi Valley Historical Review* 7 (March 1921): 363–77.

Levasseur, A. *Lafayette En Amérique, En 1824 et 1825, ou Journal D'Un Voyage aux Etats-Unis.* 2 vols. Paris: A La Librairie Baudouin, 1829.

Maury, Ann, ed. *Memoirs of a Huguenot Family.* New York: G. P. Putnam's Sons, 1853.

Sewall, Samuel. *Diary, 1674–1729.* 3 vols. Collections of the Massachusetts Historical Society, vols. 5–7, 5th ser. Boston: Massachusetts Historical Society, 1878–1882.

Stuart, John G. "A Journal Remarks or Observations In A Voyage Down the Kentucky, Ohio, Mississippi Rivers, &c." *Register of the Kentucky Historical Society* 50 (January 1952): 5–25.

VI. Miscellaneous Contemporary Works

Anderson, Adam. *An Historical and Chronological Deduction of the Origin of Commerce, from the Earliest Accounts.* 4 vols. London: J. Walter, 1787–1789.

Ashe, Thomas. *Travels in America, Performed in 1806, For the Purpose of Exploring the Rivers Alleghany, Monongahela, Ohio, and Mississippi, and Ascertaining the Produce and Condition of their Banks and Vicinity.* London: E. M. Blunt, 1808.

Beverley, Robert. *The History of Virginia, in Four Parts*. London: F. Fayram and J. Clarke, 1722.

Boucherie, Anthony. *The Art of Making Whiskey, so as to Obtain a Better, Purer, Cheaper and Greater Quantity of Spirit, from a Given Quantity of Grain: also, the Art of Converting It into Gin, after the Process of the Holland Distillers, without any Augmentation of Price*. Lexington, Ky.: Worsley and Smith, 1819.

Boydell, James, *The Ullage Cash Gauger, Comprised in a Series of Tables. . . .* London: R. and H. Causton, 1784.

Brackenridge, Hugh H. *Incidents of the Insurrection in the Western Parts of Pennsylvania, In the Year 1794*. Philadelphia: John M'Culloch, 1795.

Brickell, John. *The Natural History of North Carolina*. Dublin: James Carson, 1737.

Butler, Mann. *A History of the Commonwealth of Kentucky*. Louisville: Wilcox, Dickerman and Co., 1834.

Casseday, Ben. *The History of Louisville from Its Earliest Settlement Till the Year 1852*. Louisville: Hull and Brother, 1852.

Charless, Joseph. *Lexington Directory, Taken for Charless' Almanack, for 1806*. Lexington, Ky.: Joseph Charless, 1806.

Cist, Charles, *Cincinnati in 1841: Its Early Annals and Future Prospects*. Cincinnati: By the author, 1841.

———. *The Cincinnati Miscellany, or Antiquities of the West*. 2 vols. Cincinnati: Caleb Clark, 1845–1846.

———. *Sketches and Statistics of Cincinnati in 1859*. Cincinnati: By the author, 1859.

Collins, Lewis. *Historical Sketches of Kentucky*. Cincinnati: J. A. & U. P. James, 1847.

Cooper, A. (Distiller). *The Complete Distiller*. London: P. Valiant, 1757.

Cooper, Thomas. *Some Information Respecting America*. London: By the author, 1794.

Coxe, Tench. *A View of the United States of America*. Philadelphia: By the author, 1794.

Cramer, Zadok. *The Navigator*. Pittsburgh: By the author, 1811.

DeBow, J. D. B. *The Industrial Resources, Etc., of the Southern and Western States*. 3 vols. New Orleans: Office of *DeBow's Review*, 1852.

———. *The Southern States: Embracing a Series of Papers Condensed from the Earlier Volumes of DeBow's Review, upon*

Slavery and the Slave Institutions of the South, Internal Improvements, etc., Together with Historical and Statistical Sketches of Several of the Southern and South Western States; Their Agriculture, Commerce, etc. Washington, D.C.: By the author, 1856.

Deering, Richard. *Louisville: Her Commercial, Manufacturing and Social Advantages.* Louisville: Hanna and Co., 1859.

Feuchtwanger, Lewis. *Fermented Liquors: A Treatise on Brewing, Distilling, Rectifying, and Manufacturing of Sugars, Wines, Spirits,* . . . New York: By the author, 1858.

Filson, John. *The Discovery, Settlement and Present State of Kentucke.* Wilmington, Del.: James Adams, 1784.

Flint, Timothy. *A Condensed Geography and History of the Western States or the Mississippi Valley.* 2 vols. Cincinnati: William M. Farnsworth, 1828.

Greeley, Horace, and others. *The Great Industries of the United States.* Hartford: J. B. Burr & Hyde, 1872.

Hall, Harrison. *The Distiller.* Philadelphia: By the author, 1818.

Hariot, Thomas. *Narrative of the First English Plantation of Virginia.* London: Bernard Quaritch, 1893. (Reprint of 1588 edition.)

Imlay, Gilbert. *A Topographical Description of the Western Territory of North America.* New York: Samuel Campbell, 1793.

Jegli, John B. *Louisville, New-Albany, Jeffersonville, Shippingport and Portland Directory for 1845–1846.* Louisville: Office of the *Louisville Journal*, 1845.

Jonas, Peter. *A Complete Set of New Hydrometer Tables.* London: Thomas North, 1807.

Jones, Thomas. *The Art of Distilling Simple and Compound Waters.* London: By the author, 1820.

Krafft, Michael August. *The American Distiller, or, the Theory and Practice of Distilling, According to the Latest Discoveries and Improvements, including the Most Improved Methods of Constructing Stills, and of Rectification.* Philadelphia: Archibald Bartram, 1804.

Lawson, John. *A New Voyage to Carolina.* Edited by Hugh Talmage Lefler. Chapel Hill: University of North Carolina Press, 1967. (Original edition was 1709.)

Littell, William. *Political Transactions In and Concerning Kentucky, from the First Settlement Thereof, Until It Became an Independent State, in June, 1792.* Frankfort: William Hunter, 1806.

M'Murtrie, H. *Sketches of Louisville and Its Environs.* Louisville: S. Penn, Jun., 1819.

Marshall, Humphrey. *The History of Kentucky.* 2 vols. Frankfort: Geo. S. Robinson, 1824.

Morewood, Samuel. *A Philosophical and Statistical History of the Inventions and Customs of Ancient and Modern Nations in the Manufacture and Use of Inebriating Liquors; with the Present Practice of Distillation in all its Varieties.* Dublin: William Curry, Jr., and Co. and William Carson, 1838.

Seybert, Adam. *Statistical Annals.* Philadelphia: Thomas Dobson & Son, 1818.

Sheffield, Lord John Baker Holroyd. *Observations on the Commerce of the American States.* London: J. Debrett, 1784.

Smith, George. *A Compleat Body of Distilling, Explaining the Mysteries of that Science.* . . . London: By the author, 1738.

Smith, John. *The Generall Historie of Virginia, New-England, and the Summer Isles.* . . . London: Edward Blackmore, 1632.

Strachey, William. *The Historie of Travaile into Virginia Britannia.* London: Hakluyt Society, 1899. (Reprint of MS copy, c.1618.)

Toulmin, Harry. *A Description of Kentucky, in North America: to which are prefixed Miscellaneous Observations Respecting the United States.* London: By the author, 1792.

Trollope, Frances. *Domestic Manners of the Americans.* London: Richard Bentley, 1839.

Wansey, Henry. *An Excursion to the United States of North America, in the Summer of 1794.* Salisbury, Eng.: J. Easton, 1798.

Worth, W. Y——. *Dr. Worth's Letter in Answer to W. R. Gent.* London: By the author, 1691.

VII. Biographies and Biographical Sketches

Bakeless, John. *Daniel Boone.* Harrisburg, Pa.: Stackpole Co., 1965.

Biographical Encyclopaedia of Kentucky of the Dead and Living Men of the Nineteenth Century. Cincinnati: J. H. Armstrong and Co., 1878.

Brant, Irving. *James Madison.* 6 vols. Indianapolis: Bobbs-Merrill Co., 1941–1961.

Freeman, Douglas Southall. *George Washington.* 7 vols. New York: Charles Scribner's Sons, 1948–1957.

Haworth, Paul Leland. *George Washington, Country Gentleman.* Indianapolis: Bobbs-Merrill Co., 1925.

Hay, Thomas Robson, and Werner, M. R. *The Admirable Trumpeter: A Biography of General James Wilkinson.* Garden City, N.Y.: Doubleday, Doran and Co., 1941.

Henderson, Archibald. "Isaac Shelby, Revolutionary Patriot and Border Hero." *North Carolina Booklet* 16 (1917); 18 (1918).

Johnson, Allen, and Malone, Dumas, eds. *Dictionary of American Biography.* 20 vols. New York: Charles Scribner's Sons, 1943.

Kirwan, Albert D. *John J. Crittenden: The Struggle for the Union.* Lexington: University of Kentucky Press, 1962.

Mason, Kathryn Harrod. *James Harrod of Kentucky.* Baton Rouge: Louisiana State University Press, 1951.

Mayo, Bernard. *Henry Clay: Spokesman of the New West.* Boston: Houghton Mifflin Co., 1937.

Rives, William C. *History of the Life and Times of James Madison.* 3 vols. Boston: Little, Brown and Co., 1868–1873.

Rowland, Kate Mason. *The Life of George Mason, 1725–1792.* 2 vols. New York: G. P. Putnam's Sons, 1892.

Shreve, Royal Ornan. *The Finished Scoundrel* [General James Wilkinson]. Indianapolis: Bobbs-Merrill Co., 1933.

Talbert, Charles Gano. *Benjamin Logan: Kentucky Frontiersman.* Lexington: University of Kentucky Press, 1962.

White's Conspectus of American Biography. New York: James T. White and Co., 1937.

Wilson, James Grant, and Fiske, John, eds. *Appleton's Cyclopaedia of American Biography.* 6 vols. New York: D. Appleton and Co., 1888–1892.

Woodward, W. E. *George Washington: The Image and the Man.* New York: Boni and Liveright, 1926.

VIII. General Works and Special Studies

Ackerly, Mary Denham, and Parker, Lula Eastman Jeter. *"Our Kin": The Genealogies of Some of the Early Families Who Made History in the Founding and Development of Bedford County, Virginia.* Lynchburg: J. P. Bell Co., 1930.

Adams, Henry Carter. *Taxation in the United States, 1789–1816.*

Johns Hopkins University Studies in Historical and Political Science, vol. 2. Baltimore: Lord Baltimore Press, 1884.

Allen, William B. *A History of Kentucky*, . . . Louisville: Bradley and Gilbert, 1872.

Annual Statistical Report of the Distilled Spirits Industry, 1966. Washington: Distilled Spirits Institute, 1967.

Ardery, Julia Hoge. *Paris (Hopewell) Sesquicentennial. A Record of the One Hundred and Fiftieth Anniversary of the Founding of Bourbon's County Seat.* Paris, Ky.: Sesquicentennial Commission, 1939.

Baldwin, Leland D. *Whiskey Rebels: The Story of a Frontier Uprising.* Pittsburgh: University of Pittsburgh Press, 1939.

Banta, R. E. *The Ohio.* In *Rivers of America.* Edited by Hervey Allen and Carl Carmer. New York: Rinehart and Co., 1949.

Berry, Thomas S. *Western Prices Before 1861: A Study of the Cincinnati Market.* Harvard Economic Studies, vol. 74. Cambridge, Mass.: Harvard University Press, 1943.

Bishop, J. Leander. *A History of American Manufactures from 1608 to 1860.* 2 vols. Philadelphia: Edward Young and Co., 1864.

Bodley, Temple, and Wilson, Samuel M. *History of Kentucky.* 4 vols. Chicago: S. J. Clarke Publishing Co., 1928.

Bolles, Albert S. *The Financial History of the United States from 1789 to 1860.* New York: D. Appleton and Co., 1894.

Bourbon County Historical Scrapbook: A Record of the Celebration of the One Hundred Seventy-fifth Anniversary of the Founding of Bourbon County, Kentucky. Paris, Ky.: Bourbon County 175th Birthday Celebration Corp., 1961.

Brachvogel, John K. *Industrial Alcohol: Its Manufacture and Uses.* New York: Munn and Co., 1907.

Bradley, J. N., and Ham, Ellis M. *History of the Great Crossings Baptist Church.* Georgetown, Ky.: Great Crossings Baptist Church, 1945.

Bridenbaugh, Carl. *The Colonial Craftsman.* New York: New York University Press, 1950.

———. *Myths & Realities: Societies of the Colonial South.* New York: Atheneum, 1963.

Brown, John Mason. *The Political Beginnings of Kentucky.* Filson Club Publications, no. 6. Louisville: John P. Morton and Co., 1889.

Bruce, Philip Alexander. *Economic History of Virginia in the*

Seventeenth Century. 2 vols. New York: Macmillan Co., 1907.
———. *Institutional History of Virginia in the Seventeenth Century.* 2 vols. New York: G. P. Putnam's Sons, 1910.
Burns, Inez E. *History of Blount County, Tennessee.* Nashville: Benson Printing Co., 1957.
Carson, Gerald. *The Social History of Bourbon: An Unhurried Account of Our Star-Spangled American Drink.* New York: Dodd, Mead and Co., 1963.
Cartwright, Betty Goff Cook, and Gardiner, Lillian Johnson, comps. *North Carolina Land Grants in Tennessee, 1778–1791.* Memphis: I. C. Harper Co., 1958.
Clark, Thomas D. *A History of Kentucky.* Lexington: John Bradford Press, 1960.
Clark, Victor S. *History of Manufactures in the United States.* 3 vols. New York: McGraw-Hill Book Co., 1929.
Collins, Richard H. *History of Kentucky.* 2 vols. Covington, Ky.: Collins and Co., 1874.
Connor, R. D. W. *North Carolina: Rebuilding an Ancient Commonwealth, 1584–1925.* 4 vols. Chicago: American Historical Society, 1929.
Dunaway, Wayland F. *A History of Pennsylvania.* New York: Prentice-Hall, Inc., 1948.
Durrett, Reuben T. *Bryant's Station.* Filson Club Publications, no. 12. Louisville: John P. Morton and Co., 1897.
———. *The Centenary of Kentucky.* Filson Club Publications, no. 7. Louisville: John P. Morton and Co., 1892.
Earle, Alice Morse. *Customs and Fashions in Old New England.* New York: Charles Scribner's Sons, 1899.
Elliott, Sam Carpenter. *Nelson County Record: an Illustrated Historical and Industrial Supplement.* Bardstown, Ky.: Record Printing Co., 1896.
Emerson, Edward R. *Beverages, Past and Present.* 2 vols. New York: G. P. Putnam's Sons, 1908.
Fehlandt, August F. *A Century of Drink Reform in the United States.* Cincinnati: Jennings and Graham, 1904.
Fletcher, Stevenson Whitcomb. *Pennsylvania Agriculture and Country Life, 1640–1840.* 2 vols. Harrisburg: Pennsylvania Historical and Museum Commission, 1950.
Fuller, John. *Art of Coppersmithing.* New York: David Williams Co., 1911.
Garrison, Charles B. *Impact of the Distilled Spirits Production*

Tax on Kentucky's Economy. Report T-556. Lexington: Spindletop Research Center, 1965.

Gilpin, Alec R. *The War of 1812 in the Old Northwest.* East Lansing, Mich.: Michigan State University Press, 1958.

Gray, Lewis Cecil. *History of Agriculture in the Southern United States to 1860.* 2 vols. New York: Peter Smith, 1941.

Grossman, Harold J. *Grossman's Guide to Wines, Spirits, and Beers.* New York: Charles Scribner's Sons, 1964.

Historical Sketch of Bedford County, Virginia, 1753–1907. Lynchburg: [Privately printed, 1907].

History of the Ohio Falls Cities and Their Counties, with Illustrations and Biographical Sketches. 2 vols. Cleveland: L. A. Williams and Co., 1882.

Howe, William W. *Municipal History of New Orleans.* Johns Hopkins University Studies in Historical and Political Science, vol. 7. Baltimore: Johns Hopkins University Press, 1889.

Hu, Tun Yuan. *The Liquor Tax in the United States, 1791–1947: A History of the Internal Revenue Taxes Imposed on Distilled Spirits by the Federal Government.* Columbia University Monographs in Public Finance and National Income, no. 1. New York: Columbia University Graduate School of Business, 1950.

Jillson, Willard Rouse. *Early Kentucky Distillers, 1783–1800.* Louisville: Standard Printing Co., 1940.

Johnston, J. Stoddard, ed. *Memorial History of Louisville from Its First Settlement to the Year 1896.* 2 vols. Chicago: American Biographical Publishing Co., 1896.

Kauffman, Henry J. *Early American Copper, Tin and Brass.* New York: Medill McBride Co., 1950.

Kentish, Thomas. *The Gaugers Guide and Measurers Manual.* London: Dring and Fage, 1861.

Koontz, Louis K. *The Virginia Frontier, 1754–1763.* Johns Hopkins University Studies in Historical and Political Science, vol. 43. Baltimore: Johns Hopkins University Press, 1925.

Lathrop, Elsie. *Early American Inns and Taverns.* New York: Tudor Publishing Co., 1936.

McKee, Major Lewis W., and Bond, Lydia K. *A History of Anderson County.* Frankfort: Roberts Printing Co., 1936.

Montule, Edouard de. *Travels in America, 1816–1817.* Translated by Edward D. Seeber. Indiana University Publications, Social Science Series, no. 9. Bloomington: Indiana University Press, 1950.

Morriss, Margaret Shove. *Colonial Trade of Maryland, 1689–1715.* Johns Hopkins University Studies in Historical and Political Science, vol. 32. Baltimore: Johns Hopkins University Press, 1914.

Nettels, Curtis P. *The Emergence of a National Economy, 1775–1815.* Vol. 2 of *Economic History of the United States.* Edited by Henry David and others. New York: Holt, Rinehart and Winston, 1962.

Nixon, Joseph R. *The German Settlers in Lincoln County and Western North Carolina.* James Sprunt Historical Publications of the North Carolina Historical Society, vol. 11. Chapel Hill: University of North Carolina Press, 1912.

Parker, Coralie. *The History of Taxation in North Carolina During the Colonial Period, 1663–1776.* New York: Columbia University Press, 1928.

Pearson, C. C., and Hendricks, J. Edwin. *Liquor and Anti-Liquor in Virginia, 1619–1919.* Durham: Duke University Press, 1967.

Perkins, James H. *Annals of the West.* Cincinnati: James R. Alback, 1847.

Perrin, William Henry. *History of Bourbon, Scott, Harrison and Nicholas Counties, Kentucky.* Chicago: O. L. Baskin and Co., 1882.

———. *History of Fayette County, Kentucky.* Chicago: O. L. Baskin and Co., 1882.

Railey, W. E. *History of Woodford County.* Frankfort: Roberts Printing Co., 1928.

Ranck, George W. *Boonesborough.* Filson Club Publications, no. 16. Louisville: John P. Morton and Co., 1901.

———. *History of Lexington, Kentucky.* Cincinnati: Robert Clarke and Co., 1872.

Ripley, William Zebina. *The Financial History of Virginia, 1609–1776.* Columbia College Studies in History, Economics and Public Law, vol. 4, no. 1. New York: Columbia College, 1893.

Rogers, R. Vashon. *Drinks, Drinkers and Drinking, or the Law and History of Intoxicating Liquors.* Albany: Weed, Parsons and Co., 1881.

Roundell, Mrs. Charles. *The Still Room.* London: John Lane, 1903.

Russell, Ward. *Church Life in the Blue Grass, 1783–1933.* Lexington: Privately printed, 1933.

Rust, Ellsworth Marshall, ed. *Rust of Virginia: Genealogical and Biographical Sketches of the Descendants of William Rust, 1654–1940.* Washington: By the author, 1940.

Sandburg, Carl. *Abraham Lincoln, the Prairie Years.* 2 vols. New York: Charles Scribner's Sons, 1926.

Sanders, Robert Stuart. *An Historical Sketch of Springfield Presbyterian Church.* Frankfort: Roberts Printing Co., 1954.

———. *History of Walnut Hill Presbyterian Church.* Frankfort: Kentucky Historical Society, 1956.

Shaler, N. S. *Kentucky, A Pioneer Commonwealth.* Boston: Houghton, Mifflin and Co., 1884.

Spencer, J. H. *A History of Kentucky Baptists, from 1769 to 1885.* 2 vols. Cincinnati: Printed for the author, 1886.

Staples, Charles R. *The History of Pioneer Lexington (Kentucky), 1779–1806.* Lexington: Transylvania Press, 1939.

Steiner, Bernard C. *Western Maryland in the Revolution.* Johns Hopkins University Studies in Historical and Political Science, vol. 20. Baltimore: Johns Hopkins University Press, 1902.

Stewart, George Rippey. *Names on the Land.* New York: Random House, 1945.

Sydnor, Charles S. *Gentlemen Freeholders: Political Practices in Washington's Virginia.* Chapel Hill: University of North Carolina Press, 1952.

Taylor, John. *A History of Ten Baptist Churches.* Frankfort: J. H. Holleman, 1823.

Taylor, Oliver. *Historic Sullivan: A History of Sullivan County, Tennessee.* Bristol, Tenn.: King Printing Co., 1909.

Townsend, William H. *Lincoln and His Wife's Home Town.* Indianapolis: Bobbs-Merrill Co., 1929.

———. *Lincoln and Liquor.* New York: Press of the Pioneers, 1934.

Verhoeff, Mary. *The Kentucky River Navigation.* Filson Club Publications, no. 28. Louisville: John P. Morton and Co., 1917.

Walden, Howard T. *Native Inheritance: The Story of Corn in America.* New York: Harper and Row, 1966.

Wertenbaker, Thomas J. *The Shaping of Colonial Virginia.* New York: Russell and Russell, 1958.

Willkie, H. F. *Beverage Spirits in America: A Brief History.* New York: Newcomen Society of England (American Branch), 1949.

Woodward, Carl Raymond. *The Development of Agriculture in New Jersey, 1640–1880*. New Brunswick: Rutgers University Press, 1927.

———. *Ploughs and Politicks: Charles Read of New Jersey and His Notes on Agriculture, 1715–1774*. New Brunswick: Rutgers University Press, 1941.

IX. Articles

Anderson, Niles. "The General Chooses a Road." *Western Pennsylvania Historical Magazine* 42 (December 1959):383–401.

Barker, Charles R. "Colonial Taverns of Lower Merion." *Pennsylvania Magazine of History and Biography* 52 (1928):205–28.

Bean, Walton E. "War and the British Colonial Farmer: A Reëvaluation in the Light of New Statistical Records." *Pacific Historical Review* 11 (December 1942):439–47.

Burnett, Edmund C., comp. "Papers Relating to Bourbon County, Georgia." *American Historical Review* 15 (October 1909):66–111.

Cleland, Hugh G. "John B. C. Lucas, Physiocrat on the Frontier." *Western Pennsylvania Historical Magazine* 36 (March 1953):1–15.

Clift, G. Glenn, ed. "War of 1812 Diary of William B. Northcutt." *Register of the Kentucky Historical Society* 56 (April 1958):165–81.

Cooke, Jacob E. "The Whiskey Insurrection: A Re-evaluation." *Pennsylvania History* 30 (July 1963):316–46.

Coulter, E. Merton. "The Efforts of the Democratic Societies of the West to Open the Navigation of the Mississippi." *Mississippi Valley Historical Review* 11 (December 1924):376–89.

Dunaway, Wayland Fuller. "Pennsylvania as an Early Distributing Center for Population." *Pennsylvania Magazine of History and Biography* 55 (1931):134–69.

Fink, Paul M. "The Early Press of Jonesboro." *East Tennessee Historical Society Publications* 10 (1938):57–70.

Frantz, John B. "John C. Guldin, Pennsylvania-German Revivalist." *Pennsylvania Magazine of History and Biography* 87 (April 1963):123–38.

Gillingham, Harrold E. "Old Business Cards of Philadelphia." *Pennsylvania Magazine of History and Biography* 53 (1929): 203–29.

———. "Some Early Philadelphia Instrument Makers." *Pennsylvania Magazine of History and Biography* 51 (1927):289–308.

Gronert, Theodore G. "Trade in the Blue-Grass Region, 1810–1820." *Mississippi Valley Historical Review* 5 (December 1914):313–23.

Guffey, Alexander S. "The First Courts in Western Pennsylvania." *Western Pennsylvania Historical Magazine* 7 (July 1924): 145–77.

Harpster, John W. "Eighteenth-Century Inns and Taverns of Western Pennsylvania." *Western Pennsylvania Historical Magazine* 19 (March 1936):5–16.

"Journal of Col. John May, of Boston, Relative to a Journey to the Ohio Country, 1789." *Pennsylvania Magazine of History and Biography* 45 (1921):101–79.

McGrane, R. C., ed. "William Clark's Journal of General Wayne's Campaign." *Mississippi Valley Historical Review* 1 (December 1914):418–44.

Martin, Asa Earl. "The Temperance Movement in Pennsylvania Prior to the Civil War." *Pennsylvania Magazine of History and Biography* 49 (1925):195–230.

Matthews, Maxine. "Old Inns of East Tennessee." *East Tennessee Historical Society Publications* 2 (1930):23–33.

Nevin, Fleming. "The Liquor Question in Colonial and Revolutionary War Periods." *Western Pennsylvania Historical Magazine* 13 (July 1930):195–201.

Posey, Walter B. "The Frontier Baptist Ministry." *East Tennessee Historical Society Publications* 14 (1942):3–10.

Quaife, M. M., ed. "A Narrative of the Northwestern Campaign of 1813, by Stanton Sholes." *Mississippi Valley Historical Review* 15 (March 1929):519–25.

Randall, James G. "George Rogers Clark's Service of Supply." *Mississippi Valley Historical Review* 8 (December 1921): 250–63.

Rogers, William Flinn. "Life in East Tennessee Near End of Eighteenth Century." *East Tennessee Historical Society Publications* 1 (1929):27–42.

Schmidt, Otto L., ed. "The Mississippi Valley in 1816 through an Englishman's Diary." *Mississippi Valley Historical Review* 14 (September 1927): 137–55.

Silveus, Marian. "Churches and Social Control on the Western Pennsylvania Frontier." *Western Pennsylvania Historical Magazine* 19 (June 1936): 123–34.

Wallace, Carson W. "Transportation and Traffic on the Ohio and the Mississippi before the Steamboat." *Mississippi Valley Historical Review* 7 (June 1920): 26–38.

Williams, Edward G., ed. "The Orderly Book of Colonel Henry Bouquet's Expedition Against the Ohio Indians, 1764." *Western Pennsylvania Historical Magazine* 42 (September 1959): 283–302.

Winston, James E. "Notes on the Economic History of New Orleans, 1803–1836." *Mississippi Valley Historical Review* 11 (September 1924): 200–226.

Index

Acrelius, Israel, 14
Adulteration of whiskey: in colonial America, 12–13; legislation against, 13, 35
Aging: factor in whiskey quality, 109, 110; importance of, 109, 110, 111, 112; early method of, 110; advantages of, 127, 127 n; "Old Bourbon," 127, 128; requirements, 128
Agricultural fairs, 115, 116, 117
American Revolution, 52
Anchor, 45, 45 n
Anderson, Colonel Alexander, 55 n
Areometers, 108, 109
Armstrong, Captain John, 65–66
Arthur, John, 99, 99 n
Artificial spirits, 120; recipes for, 133
Ashe, Thomas, 7–8
Auglaize River, 66, 66 n

Bachelors Joy, 80–81
Bacon, Roger, 1
Bailey, Captain John, 64–65
Baker, Isaac, 23–24, 24 n
Baldwin, Thomas, 62
Baltimore, Maryland, 20, 52
Baptist ministers, 69
Bardstown, 51, 111
Barr, Robert, 50–51
Barrels: specifications, 129, 130, 133; charred inner surface, 129, 130, 131, 132, 133, 135; probable origin of charring process, 130–31; double barrels, 130, 132
Bartan, Daniel, 30

Barton, Michal, 111
Baxter, German, 51
Bean's Station, Tennessee, 21, 21 n
Beatty, C., and Co., 53
Bedford, John, 122
Bedford County, Virginia, 31, 138
Beer breweries, 91
Bertie County, North Carolina, 10
Bethabara, 19
Beverley, Robert, 4
Bishop, J. Leander, 5, 6
Black's Fort, 33
Blair, Samuel, 29
Blue Licks, Battle of, 138
Bodley, Temple, 93
Bodley, Major Thomas, 65, 66
Boilers, steam, 55, 56
Boone, Colonel Daniel, 23, 38
Boone, Squire, 38, 138
Boonesborough, Kentucky, 24, 26, 27, 62
Boonsfort. *See* Boonesborough
Boston, Massachusetts, 52
Bosworth, Benajah, 119
Botetourt County, Virginia, 33
Boucherie, Anthony, 59–60, 108, 109
Bourbon Agricultural Society, 116
Bourbon County, Georgia, 124 n
Bourbon County, Kentucky, early distilling in, xi; no active distilleries at present, xi; creation of, 46, 46 n, 124 n, 125; first court convened, 46; and tax collection, 88, 92, 100 n; agricultural fairs, 117, 132; original size, 125; men-

165

INDEX